...ed to write a ...worth for 46 years ...g in these parts and what it means to so many to get out of the towns and see what happens in this beautiful part of the country that is so near to them.

Gillian takes you through some of the most interesting villages, where you will find you will have to stop to look inside the churches, some of which are remarkable, and try the cafés on the way.

The Hospice movement, especially when it is directed to very ill children, is one which must be kept going and it relies so much on charitable donations.

To complete the 35 mile walk with the backing of friends and relations and using this book as a guide will raise money to help the Bluebell Wood Children's Hospice continue to do its important work.

With all good wishes to those who walk and read this book.

Deborah Devonshire

The Dowager Duchess of Devonshire
Photo: Bridget Flemming

Sam Scotford   *Tom Scotford*

Contents

Dedications

My inspiration for writing this book comes from my precious, beautiful son Thomas and all the children of Bluebell Wood Children's Hospice.

"The Golden Miles" is dedicated to my Mum and Dad who gave me a lovely childhood, my husband Russell, my boys who continually make me appreciate life, my lovely family and my dear friend Giovanna.

Finally, to Si Homfray, a very kind and gentle man who made this book possible.

Author's Note:

Author: Gillian Scotford
Publishers: Hammer Design, Heather Lane
                 Hathersage, S32 1DP
                 Tel: 01433 650555
                 Email: info@hammerdesign.co.uk
Distribution: Mayfield Books, Sheffield
                 Tel: 0800 834920
                 Email: sales@mayfield-books.co.uk
Printers: J W Northend Ltd, Sheffield
ISBN: 9781902674315

The detailed contents of this book are believed to be accurate at the time of compilation. Gillian Scotford cannot accept responsibility for any omissions or errors or for changes in any details provided. The information is intended only as a guide. Prior to booking any accommodation it is advisable that you contact the proprietor to confirm the walking distance from the starting points in each village. In order to ensure that "The Golden Miles" Route only recommends accommodation with high standards and service levels, every effort was made during this compilation to research compliance with industry standards and "star" ratings. However, these standards and ratings are subject to review on an annual basis and I suggest that prior to booking you check the current status of accommodation to ensure that it meets YOUR standards. Accommodation, fine dining and refreshment centres are dynamic segments of the tourist industry. Local tourist information centres will provide details of recent enterprise.

Sunset over Owler Tor
Photo: Karen Frenkel

A 35 mile walk - through the most beautiful English Countryside.

For your own charity challenge or purely for pleasure take 2 days or 2 weeks - just dive in and enjoy!

'Destination of Distinction'

With 32.7 million day visitors per year and Derbyshire having recently been selected as a 'Destination of Distinction' by Visit England... "The Golden Miles" offers a series of truly special locations for everyone to enjoy.

The fleeting hour of life of those who love the hills is quickly spent, but the hills are eternal. Always there will be the lonely ridge, the dancing beck, the silent forest; always there will be the exhilaration of the summits. These are for the seeking, and those who seek and find while there is yet time will be blessed both in mind and body

Alfred Wainwright, The Western Fells

Children's Hospices UK

Few of us with healthy children will ever appreciate fully the devastation on hearing that your child is either profoundly disabled or suffering from a life threatening or life limiting condition.

At that moment the hopes and dreams of the parents are shattered by the realisation that their pride and joy is unlikely to reach adulthood. It isn't long before the reality sinks in regarding the huge physical, emotional and financial challenges that lie ahead in providing care and support 24 hours a day, 7 days a week, 52 weeks a year for the foreseeable future.

It is estimated that at any given time 25,000 families throughout the United Kingdom are caught up in these tragic circumstances with variable outcomes from infant death to gradual deterioration over several years.

The majority of these families face their trauma without the facilities and support of a children's hospice. In the United Kingdom there are just 40 children's hospices providing a unique range of services including respite care and end of life care for the whole family.

Bluebell Wood Childrens Hospice

EXPRESSED QUITE SIMPLY, AT THIS MOMENT THERE ARE ONLY 269 CHILDREN'S HOSPICE BEDS THROUGHOUT THE UK, PROVIDING ALL LEVELS OF HOSPICE BASED CARE! WHICH CLEARLY IS NOWHERE NEAR SUFFICIENT TO MEET THE DEMAND.

The word hospice, if not stigmatised is often misconstrued as merely a place where terminally ill patients spend their last few days. The truth is that they are usually places where fun and laughter is infectious and where dedicated teams of professional carers make sure that the families make the most of their lives.

Time and space is provided where the families can meet together in a relaxed environment and share their concerns and fears. In the context of respite care the family is able, albeit briefly, to set aside the household chores and concentrate on each other.

Typically, a children's hospice will cost £5,000,000 to build and equip, all of which has to be raised by local voluntary and charitable organisations. Once

Above: The Bluebell Girls at Thornbridge Hall celebrating a successful walk

completed and accredited, the annual running costs amount to approximately £2,500,000 of which only a small variable amount (12.5% in the case of Bluebell Wood) is funded by central government, leaving £2,187,500 to be raised each year by local charities.

Systematic and consistent fundraising is essential to maintain the current level of service provision. Determined campaigning and lobbying of government by the children's hospice movement is vital, especially in the current economic climate, until a more equitable division of responsibility is achieved.

These deserving families should reasonably expect to receive quality care and support close to their homes. The dedicated teams of health care professionals and carers can make a REAL difference.

"The Golden Miles" Route book will hopefully contribute to the debate by highlighting the need for more children's hospices in the UK. At the same time it should bring pleasure to many families by encouraging them to visit The Peak District and enjoy some of the most beautiful scenery in the country.

Emma Harrison CBE

Emma Harrison CBE – Group Chairman of A4e (Action for Employment)

Top: Dawn over the White Peak
Photo: Karen Frenkel

Above: Gillian, megaphone and Tom 2010
Photo: Sheffield Newspapers Ltd

Above Right: Bluebell Girls set off
Photo: Sheffield Newspapers Ltd

Right: Alex Ritchie piping the Bluebell Girls 2010
Photo: Sheffield Newspapers Ltd

The inspiration for "The Golden Miles" came from a 35 mile circular walk through 20 Derbyshire villages that I originated to increase awareness of, and to raise funds for, The Bluebell Wood Children's Hospice at North Anston, near Sheffield.

My beautiful son Thomas, is one of 500 children with limited life expectancy who require the facilities of the hospice as part of their routine care. The initiative became known as 'Tom's Golden Mile Challenge' and the walk is now established as an annual event in the hospice's fundraising calendar.

The aim of my book is to share the route and our experiences with as wide an audience as possible together with a feature on each of the 20 Derbyshire villages.

Each section contains a concise data file with contact details for hotels, restaurants, attractions and local transport details, all designed to make your stay in The Peak District as convenient and pleasurable as possible.

The walk is completed leisurely over three days in June each year but by all means spread it over a week – you could then be sure of a fantastic time exploring these beautiful villages.

Serious walkers and members of The Long Distance Walking Association may wish to complete the 35 miles within the day! For those wishing to take their tent along, there are several camp sites en route where you would be most welcome!

Simply choose any village as the starting point and use "The Golden Miles" Route as a reference book to plan your itinerary, accommodation, meals and refreshment.

Just as a suggestion, if you're coming to the area by train you may wish to choose Hathersage or Grindleford as your starting point.

You may notice that I describe various parts of The Peak District as 'the best place ever' and that we appear to be eating and drinking Peak District delights all along the route. Well, the truth is that The Peak District IS one of the most beautiful parts of the United Kingdom and Yes, we did!

6 Shorter Walks:

I have divided the route into 6 shorter walks for those who would like to enjoy only a part of "The Golden Miles" route or who wish to book one holiday accommodation for the duration of their stay and use their car to drive to the starting points of the 6 shorter walks.

Jamie Oliver meets the boys at the Hospice

Bluebell Wood Children's Hospice

My name is Gillian Scotford and I am married to Russell and we have 3 beautiful children, Max 17, Thomas 15 and Sam 12. Max is fit and well, Thomas is severely brain damaged, prone to fits and choking, has had 3 respiratory arrests and requires 24-hour care. Sam had a stroke during pregnancy and suffers from cerebral palsy.

Within a very short period of time our family life had changed dramatically and completely. It became increasingly clear that we needed a highly specialised team to provide respite and to support the whole family practically and emotionally during the many crises. Bluebell Wood Children's Hospice cares for the children of North Derbyshire, South Yorkshire, North Lincolnshire and North Nottinghamshire with life threatening or life limiting illnesses.

For a number of years, I was a District Nursing Sister providing nursing care throughout the 20 towns and villages along "The Golden Miles" Route. I discovered that amongst healthcare professionals and others providing the support matrix for children requiring 24 hour care, the role of the hospice movement is usually misunderstood and stigmatised. The perception of a hospice is that of a place where patients are sent to spend their last few days in a protected environment with all the associated concerns and fears. Accordingly, referral of a child to the hospice was frequently and inappropriately delayed.

The reality is quite different. Bluebell Wood is often a joyful and laughter filled place where the most caring and considerate aspects of human nature are in evidence.

My family considers that we are one of the fortunate 500 whose critical and respite care are covered by the facilities at The Bluebell Wood Children's Hospice. It is a sobering thought that with a derisory 12.5% contribution from central government towards the £2,500,000 annual running costs, £2,187,500 must be raised from local charitable organisations to maintain that level of care and support.

The hope is that by compiling this book I can in some small way raise awareness of the fantastic work of The Bluebell Wood Children's Hospice and their need for continual financial support from the local community. All the profits from this initiative will be directed to those precious children and their families who desperately need specialist care. I can assure you that the staff at Bluebell Wood are completely dedicated to their work and so special. Metaphorically, they wrap their arms around the whole family and make you feel that somehow you will cope, whatever the outcome.

Supporting Bluebell Wood Children's Hospice

"Living with Love and Laughter" summarises the ethos of Bluebell Wood - with your commitment and financial assistance we can help to maintain their desire.

Gillian Scotford

Bluebell Wood
CHILDREN'S HOSPICE
www.bluebellwood.org

Bluebell Wood Children's Hospice Shop, now open at 5 King Street, Bakewell

Visit Bluebell Wood Children's Hospice Shop at 5 King Street, Bakewell. Selling the best in second hand goods and a range of stylish new goods, the shop also has a second floor bookshop with comfy chairs and tea and coffee facilities.

Bluebell Wood
CHILDREN'S HOSPICE

Opening Hours

Monday - Saturday   9.00am - 4.30pm
Sunday   10.00am - 4.30pm

Do you have unwanted items to donate? Just drop them into the shop during opening hours or if you have more than 10 bags to donate, call 01909 517 360 and we'll pick them up for you.

Can't get to the Bakewell shop? A selection of our products are available online at www.bluebellwood.org

About Bluebell Wood

Bluebell Wood Children's Hospice provides care to children with life-threatening conditions, who aren't expected to reach adulthood. Our hospice is a place filled with love and laughter where families can relax and have a break, knowing that their child is being cared for.

There are only 40 children's hospices in the country, and Bluebell Wood covers all of South Yorkshire, North Derbyshire, North Nottinghamshire and North East Lincolnshire. It costs £2.5 million every year to provide this care, and with no statutory government funding, without our supporters we simply couldn't help all the children that we do.

For more information on how you could help Bluebell Wood Children's Hospice, go to www.bluebellwood.org

The Richard Foundation.
Bluebell Wood Children's Hospice, Cramfit Road, North Anston S25 4AJ Telephone 01909 517 360.
www.bluebellwood.org
A company limited by guarantee no. 03809663.
Registered Charity No. 1076958.

Bluebell Wood
CHILDREN'S HOSPICE

The Golden Miles Countryside Code

- Keep dogs under close control
- Guard against fire
- Please use gates and stiles on the walks – close and fasten all gates after using them
- Take litter home
- Protect wildlife and trees
- Consider other people
- Take special care on country roads
- Be safe – plan ahead and follow any signs
- Make no unnecessary noise
- Enjoy the countryside
- Ensure you are wearing suitable clothing and footwear
- If possible, always tell someone your intended route
- Take a good supply of provisions
- Be aware of mineshafts remaining from the lead mining in the area. Whilst most have been capped, all are in a hazardous condition due to age
- It is recommended you use an Ordnance Survey 1:25,000 map to accompany "The Golden Miles"

Sponsors and Advertisers

Thanks go to the businesses and individuals who have made the production of this walking guide possible. There are a number of advertisements throughout the guide and in addition there are some highlighted businesses in the listings pages as thanks for their contributions.

Legend

Road		Steps	
Path		Built Areas	
Coniferous and non-coniferous wooded areas		Caravan Park	
Farm		Camping	
Sleeping Accommodation		Pub	
360 degree views		Telephone	
180 degree views		School	
Bluebells		Cricket Pitch	
Golf Course		Route of walk	
Cottages with gardens		Start & finish	
Church		Fields	
Café - Tea room		Grazing Animals	
Toilets		Hang Gliders	
		Parking	

① - ⑥ Starting point of 6 shorter walks (return routes)

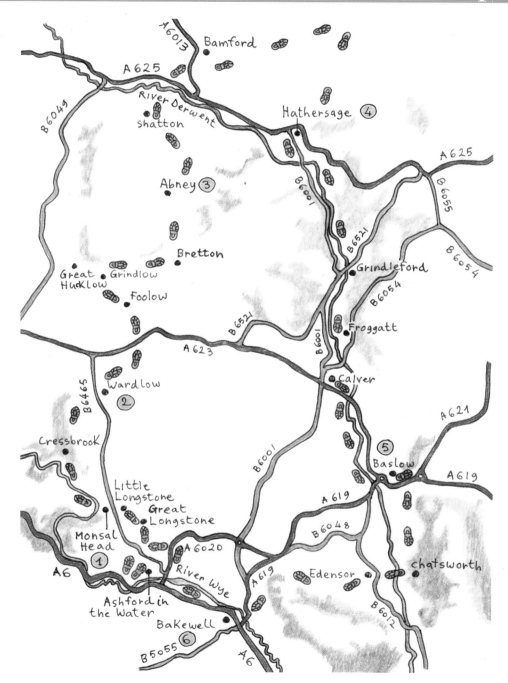

Abney Low from Eyam Moor
Photo: Graham Dunn

Hathersage from Surprise View
Photo: Graham Dunn

Bakewell
Photo: Graham Dunn

Froggatt Edge
Photo: Graham Dunn

Monsal Dale
Photo: Graham Dunn

Field near Monsal Head
Photo: Graham Dunn

The six shorter walks

I have divided the route into 6 shorter walks for those who would like to enjoy only a part of "The Golden Miles" route or who wish to book one holiday accommodation for the duration of their stay and use their car to drive to the starting points of the 6 shorter walks.

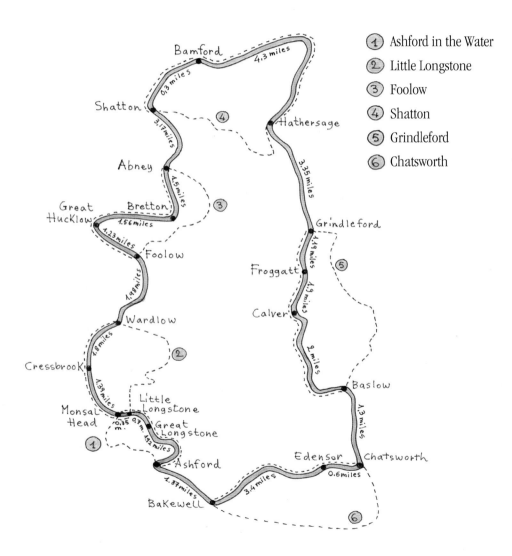

1. Ashford in the Water
2. Little Longstone
3. Foolow
4. Shatton
5. Grindleford
6. Chatsworth

Public Transport

The Peak District has an excellent rural public transport network.

General Information:
Traveline	www.traveline.org.uk	Tel: 08712 002233

Trains:
National Rail Enquires	www.nationalrail.co.uk	Tel: 08457 484950
East Midlands Trains	www.eastmidlandstrains.co.uk	Tel: 08457 125678
Northern Rail	www.northernrail.org	

Buses and Coaches:
Derbyshire Buses	www.derbyshire.gov.uk/buses	
National Express	www.nationalexpress.com	
Transpeak bus service	www.trentbarton.co.uk	
Peakconnections	www.visitpeakdistrict.com/peakconnections	
TM Travel	www.tmtravel.co.uk	Tel: 01142 633890
Hulleys of Baslow	www.hulleys-of-baslow.co.uk	Tel: 01246 582246

Bus and Train Travel:
Derbyshire Wayfarer day rover ticket offers virtually unlimited travel for a day.
www.derbyshire.gov.uk

A new service linked with Virgin Trains is to be available bringing tourists from St Pancras to Bakewell

Useful Websites

www.weathercall.co.uk
www.visitpeakdistrict.com
www.peakdistrict.gov.uk
www.qualityintourism.com
www.theaa.com
www.thenationaltrust.org.uk

Tourist Information

Tourist Information Centre, Bakewell Visitor Centre, The Old Market Hall, Bridge Street, Bakewell DE45 1DS

Tel: 01629 813227
Web: www.peakdistrict.gov.uk
Email: bakewell@peakdistrict.gov.uk

For up to date information for local markets, events, well dressings and festivals throughout the 20 villages, please visit **www.visitpeakdistrict.com**

Private Hire

Pacman Travel (Bakewell)	8 seater minibus - luggage service and taxi hire	Tel: 07971 400015
S.O.S. Taxi (Hathersage)	8 Seater minibus - luggage service and taxi hire	Tel: 07541 101076
Andrews of Tideswell	Luxury transport for 8 - 78 people www.andrews-of-tideswell.co.uk	Tel: 01298 871222
Hulleys of Baslow	24, 49 or 53 seater coaches available by private charter www.hulleys-of-baslow.co.uk	Tel: 01246 582246

If you decide to book a cottage in one of the villages for a week in order to have a base for your luggage and vehicle, public transport or private taxis may prove to be useful and cost effective additional resources. The convenience of these forms of transport may be especially beneficial if you have a young family.

There are many local taxi companies but Andrews of Tideswell (see above) is one well established minibus hire company that can be booked in advance.

Caravan/Campsites

Grindlow
(inbetween Foolow and Great Hucklow)

Derbyshire Hills Campsite, Annes Cottage, Grindlow, Nr Buxton, Derbyshire SK17 8RJ

Tel: 07935 480444

www.derbyshirehills.co.uk

Bamford
Swallowholme Caravan Park, Station Road, Bamford, Alstonefield, Hope Valley

Tel: 01433 650981

Hathersage
North Lees Campsite, Birley Lane, Hathersage, Derbyshire S33 1BR

Tel: 01433 650838

Calver
Stocking Farm Campsite, Stocking Farm, Calver, Bakewell, Derbyshire S30 1XA

Tel: 01433 630516

Baslow
Eric Byne Campsite, Moorside Farm, Birchen Edge, Baslow DE45 1NA

Tel: 01246 582277

Chatsworth
Chatsworth Park Caravan Club Site, Baslow, Bakewell, Derbyshire DE45 1PN

Tel: 01246 582226

Bakewell
Greenhills, Crowhill Lane, Bakewell DE45 1PX

Tel: 01629 813052

www.greenhillsleisure.com

Youth Hostel Associations

Bakewell, Bretton and Hathersage

Edale from the air Photo: Heath and Heaven, Living Art

Large Groups

Large Groups may consider the following self-catering accommodation

Rowdale	Ashford in the water
Churchdale Farm	Ashford in the water
Longstone Barns	Little Longstone
Cressbrook Hall	Cressbrook
Peak District Holiday Barn	Wardlow Mires
Brosterfield Farm Peak District Holiday Cottages	Foolow
Shatton Hall Farm	Shatton
Sladen Lodge	Hathersage
The Old Bakehouse	Calver
Bakewell Holiday Apartments	Bakewell

Activities in the Peak District

A variety of outdoor activities are available within the Peak District, if you wish to extend your stay and spend a few nights in one area.

Hot Air Balloon

Dragon Balloon Company
Mam House Farm, Castleton, Hope Valley, Derbyshire S33 8WA
Tel: 01433 623007
Email: info@dragonballoon.co.uk
www.dragonballoon.co.uk

Helicopter Flights

Pennine Helicopters Ltd
Oakdene Farm, Saddleworth, Greater Manchester OL3 5LU
Tel: 01457 820152
www.penninehelis.co.uk

Climbing

Abseiling Derbyshire
67 Brookfields Road, Ipstones, Staffordshire Moorlands ST10 2LY
Tel: 0800 3581307
www.abseilingderbyshire.co.uk

Peak Mountain Training
Tel: 01143 602814
www.peakmountaintraining.co.uk

Adventure Expeditions
Tel: 01305 813107
www.adventure-expeditions.net

Foundry Mountain Activities
Tel: 0845 644 5161
www.greatadventures.co.uk

Cycling

Derwent Cycle
Derwent Bamford, Hope Valley, S33 0AQ
Tel: 01433 651261
*New cycle centre opening

Hassop Station Café
Hassop Station, Bakewell, Derbyshire DE45 1NW
Tel: 01629 815 668
www.hassopstation.co.uk

MONSAL TUNNELS TO OPEN SPRING 2011, LINKING BAKEWELL TO BUXTON

Electric Bicycle Network
New to the Peak District 2011 - Various hire points available
www.electricbicyclenetwork.com

Equestrian

Ladybooth Equestrian Centre
Nether Booth, Edale, Hope Valley, Derbyshire S33 7ZH
Tel: 01433 670205
Email: info@ladybooth.co.uk
www.ladybooth.co.uk

Outdoor Activities

Peak Pursuits Ltd
Castle Hill, Nantwich Rd, Audley, Staffordshire ST7 8DH
Tel: 01782 722226
www.peakpursuits.co.uk

Chocolate Workshop

Cocoadance
Mam Farm, Castleton, Hope Valley S33 8WA
Tel: 01433 621334
www.cocoadance.com

Golf

Bakewell Golf Course
Station Road, Bakewell DE45 1GB
Tel: 01629 812307
www.bakewellgolfclub.co.uk

Sickleholme Golf Club
Bamford, Derbyshire S33 0BN
Tel: 01433 651306
www.sickleholme.co.uk

Caving

Speedwell Cavern
Winnats Pass, Castleton, Hope Valley, Derbyshire, S33 8WA
Tel: 01433 620512
www.speedwellcavern.co.uk

Treak Cliff Cavern
Buxton Road, Castleton, Hope Valley, Derbyshire, S33 8WP
Tel: 01433 620571
www.bluejohnstone.com

Blue John
Buxton Road, Castleton, Hope Valley, Derbyshire, S33 8WP
Tel: 01433 620638
www.bluejohn-cavern.co.uk

Peak Cavern
Castleton, Hope Valley, Derbyshire, S33 8WS
Tel: 01433 620285
www.peakcavern.co.uk

Spa Days

Losehill House Hotel & Spa
Edale Road, Hope, Derbyshire, S33 6RF
Tel: 01433 621219
www.losehillhouse.co.uk

Froggatt Edge Photo: Heath and Heaven, Living Art

Monsal Weir Photo: Karen Frenkel

On leaving Ashford-in-the-Water, one of the most picturesque villages of the Peak District, the walk takes us through the pretty meadows to meet the Monsal Trail, the old railway line.

After walking through Little Longstone, the home of the olde worlde Packhorse Inn, famous for its fine ales and log fires, moments later you will experience the breathtaking views of the viaduct at Monsal Head. Enjoy the food, ice creams, coffee, roaring log fire or just sit and simply take a deep breath and enjoy the pure beauty of the stepping stones, rolling hills and peace that lie before you.

The walk then leaves the famous viewpoint, and drops down onto the viaduct along the Monsal Trail and then climbs up out of Cressbrook Dale with spectacular views of the open expanse of the valley – a great stop for a picnic.

As you pass through Wardlow, a gentle relaxing stroll takes you through fields and over stiles as you gaze at the many sheep huddled together.

As we approach the village of Foolow, you can see the Barrel Inn at Bretton, the highest pub in Derbyshire perched on the edge like an oasis in the desert.

The Bulls Head at Foolow is renowned for its fine food and pretty location. With its quaint cottages and duck pond, it is exactly how you would imagine a typical English village.

The route then takes you to the village of Great Hucklow and then rises to skim under the edge to arrive at the Barrel Inn. I can honestly say I have never experienced a pub with such an unchanged and timeless cosy welcome as this. It doesn't matter whether you are the first customer of the day, alone, with a crowd or amidst the busy regulars of the Boxing Day gathering it has always provided the warmest of welcomes. Dating back to 1597 and laying claim to being the highest pub in Derbyshire, on a clear day it is possible to see 5 counties.

The crackling, glowing red coal fire is always lit, and the deep colours, brass and old ornaments make you want to

order an Irish coffee or mulled wine and sit feeling relaxed and fulfilled at your great achievements. Watching the massive red sunset, staying in the great accommodation or eating the big hearty full English breakfast all keep the residents extremely happy.

As you leave Bretton, the route enters the steep valley between Bretton and Abney. Tiny steps descend into a wonderland. This is such a pretty spot to have a picnic or a flask of coffee and biscuit near the small wooden bridge. The village of Abney is a pretty hamlet without shops or pubs but high up with fantastic, panoramic views. I would imagine if you were an Artist or Writer and wanted tranquility, this would be the place to live.

On the top of the Moors, you get a great feeling of having reached a spot that noone else has discovered! The dramatic distant rocks of the well-known Stanage Edge, Derwent Dams and the purple heather spreading far and wide, make you want to grab the best camera in the world and capture the image forever. This is another great location for a picnic. Spread a large blanket and lay on the spongy purple heather, gazing up at the passing sky, hopefully with the warm English sun melting your cares away.

I realised after doing my 35-mile walk everywhere was a great place to stop and every place we had refreshments was the most beautiful place in the world! The truth is we have so many on our doorstep.

The walk descends down to Offerton Hall with outstanding views. A well-defined path takes you down to the river and then gently meanders along the riverbank to arrive at Shatton. This is another location without shops or pubs but boasts great properties that most of us could only ever dream of living in. This section between Bretton and Shatton is without refreshment stops or toilet facilities so remember to bring your flask and toileting has to be 'Au Naturel!'

Passing the Bamford Garden Centre with refreshments and toilet facilities, we then start a section which I feel is outstanding. On my walk I had arranged champagne, sandwiches and cakes at the top so I would suggest you pop a little bottle and a plastic glass in your backpack so that you can enjoy the same treat.

The path rises up the edge of the Sickleholme Golf Course, where peace and tranquility is needed at all times. Here is the type of moment where you would never want to get on another plane ever again, when here, on your doorstep, you have unbeatable scenery. I always knew when I reached the top with the best views of the climbers' paradise, Stanage Edge, and the perfect village of Hathersage

beneath, that I would have a tear in my eye. As we had a toast to all the children with life threatening and life limiting illnesses and my friends sang 'Lean on me' in perfect harmony, it is one of those moments I will never ever forget.

The route then descends through the absolute best in British countryside, buttercups, pheasants, grazing sheep huddling around their feeding troughs and lambs springing up and down in the air. Little John's Grave, The Scotsman's Pack, David Mellor Cutlery, The Plough Inn and the famous traditional outdoor swimming baths are just some of the pleasures awaiting you in the village of Hathersage. This is a great place to stay over and just rest for one or two days. With plenty to do and lovely little local walks, it makes a great base for an English holiday with the Hathersage station nearby.

It is then time to follow the river as it gently meanders towards the village of Grindleford.

As you leave the station and cross the main road, one of the most beautiful settings is before you. The

Maynard Hotel, recently refurbished, but retaining the same elegance that it has always had, provides a great venue for whatever the occasion. With the posh bedrooms and dining room overlooking the view, you can sit around the lovely wooden furniture on the patio and just enjoy the spread of lush green before you in the garden. As we listened to the trickle of the water feature and sipped champagne, we gazed over at the distant farm on the hillside where my mum was privileged to spend her childhood.

The walk then passes the church, and before the bridge, you enter a field that has a footpath that passes beneath Froggatt Edge. Froggatt Edge is so fantastic and has been a photographers dream for many years. My walk is generally so easy underfoot for a fit family to enjoy.

The village of Froggatt is such a picturesque village with pretty gardens and cottages. The path then enters the wood and you have a feeling that you're in the storybook Narnia. As the tall forest pines give shade or shelter,

Monsal Dale Photo: Karen Frenkel

the river provides a sense of peace as it gently flows alongside you as you walk along. Leaving the wood, you walk towards the caravan site and Calver Mill. Here is a great place for refreshments at the Bridge Inn or the Calver Café and Craft Centre.

The path then goes on to follow the general line of the river Derwent into Baslow. As you walk through the field and dependent on the time of year you can appreciate the seasonal variation in flora. When we first participated in the walk, the whole field was full of small yellow flowers with the backdrop of Froggatt Edge behind you. In the wood, the pretty sight of youthful bluebells escorted us through the trees. As you enter the clear skies Curbar Edge entertains you with its beauty. The crags of Curbar Edge attract thousands of walkers and climbers all year round and whatever the weather, the path that runs along the escarpments guarantees extensive views.

I remember reading a country magazine once and it voted the walk up there as one of the most romantic walks in Britain! Our walk gazes up at this and on joining Bubnell Lane we

Millstone in Padley Gorge
Photo: Karen Frenkel

followed this to the bridge and then crossed over to the village of Baslow (Curbar, Baslow and Froggatt Edge is included in Short Walk No 5).

Baslow is a very popular village for tourists. Not only is it full of great places to eat and stay, including the famous Fischers of Baslow, but also it feels to me like the gateway to the Peak District from the M1 at Chesterfield and Sheffield. My favourite family place in the whole wide world is the Chatsworth Estate. From Baslow you can walk over the small bridge next to the village green

35 Mile Route Distances

Ashford-in-the-Water to Great Longstone	1.92 miles	Shatton to Bamford	0.30 miles
Great Longstone to Little Longstone	0.70 miles	Bamford to Hathersage	4.30 miles
Little Longstone to Monsal Head	0.35 miles	Hathersage to Grindleford	3.35 miles
Monsal Head to Cressbrook	1.39 miles	Grindleford to Froggatt	1.19 miles
Cressbrook to Wardlow	1.80 miles	Froggatt to Calver	1.90 miles
Wardlow to Foolow	1.98 miles	Calver to Baslow	2.00 miles
Foolow to Great Hucklow	1.23 miles	Baslow to Chatsworth	1.30 miles
Great Hucklow to Bretton	1.56 miles	Chatsworth to Edensor	0.60 miles
Bretton to Abney	1.50 miles	Edensor to Bakewell	3.46 miles
Abney to Shatton	3.17 miles	Bakewell to Ashford-in-the-Water	1.87 miles

Storm over Stanage Edge Photo: Karen Frenkel

and enter through the 'kissing gate' into a landscape that has stood still for hundreds of years. Children can be free to run and laugh without the fear of traffic, as this path follows the river towards the house. Whatever the season, whatever the weather, Chatsworth House has something of interest for everyone.

The path ascends with the most incredible views of Chatsworth House behind. In the evening the window frames all light up with gold as the sun sets. As you drop down over the hill, the picture postcard village of

Edensor awaits you. Every house has a bewildering array of architectural features and no two houses are alike and all set within this gated, walled, enclosed village. As you walk towards the church across the traditional English green, you can call for refreshments in the quaint tearoom. The path then ascends high up, with panoramic views of the surrounding countryside, before descending into the famous market town of Bakewell. Bakewell is so full of wonderful shops, restaurants and accommodation; you could spend a week here and not get bored.

For the final stretch of our 35 miles, the path follows the river, across the green meadows into Ashford In The Water. Pretty blossom trees and a white swan entertained us as we strolled along, feeling absolutely proud that we had found such a beautiful walk. I can honestly say that throughout my life I have enjoyed walking in the Peak District, but somehow I feel that Tom's Golden Miles Challenge has put all the best bits together and created the PERFECT GOLDEN MILES!

6 Shorter Walks Distances

Short walk 1: Ashford-in-the-Water	5.1 miles
Short walk 2: Little Longstone	6.8 miles
Short walk 3: Foolow	8.6 miles
Short walk 4: Shatton	7.8 miles
Short walk 5: Grindleford	10.1 miles
Short walk 6: Chatsworth	8.35 miles

I have put together a few different itineraries for the main 35 mile route, should you wish to take longer than we did over the three days.

2 DAY WALK

Starting Point:	Great Longstone Village
Walk Day 1:	Great Longstone to Hathersage (18.28 miles)
Walk Day 2:	Hathersage to Great Longstone (17.59 miles)

Overnight accommodation:
Day 1: Hathersage

3 DAY WALK

Starting Point:	Ashford-in-the-Water village
Walk Day 1:	Ashford-in-the-Water to Bretton (10.93 miles)
Walk Day 2:	Bretton to Grindleford (12.62 miles)
Walk Day 3:	Grindleford to Ashford-in-the-Water (12.32 miles)

Overnight accommodation:
Day 1:	Bretton
Day 2:	Grindleford

4 DAY WALK

Starting Point:	Hathersage village
Walk Day 1:	Hathersage to Baslow (8.44 miles)
Walk Day 2:	Baslow to Great Longstone (9.15 miles)
Walk Day 3:	Great Longstone to Bretton (9.01 miles)
Walk Day 4:	Bretton to Hathersage (9.27 miles)

Overnight accommodation:
Day 1:	Baslow
Day 2:	Great Longstone
Day 3:	Bretton

5 DAY WALK

Starting Point:	Bamford village
Walk day 1:	Bamford to Grindleford (7.65 miles)
Walk day 2:	Grindleford to Baslow (5.09 miles)
Walk day 3:	Baslow to Ashford-in-the-Water (7.23 miles)
Walk day 4:	Ashford-in-the-Water to Foolow (8.14 miles)
Walk day 5:	Foolow to Bamford (7.76 miles)

Overnight accommodation:
Day 1:	Grindleford
Day 2:	Baslow
Day 3:	Ashford-in-the-Water
Day 4:	Foolow

Choose your accommodation

Note : Simply choose one of the available accommodations in the selected village and if you wish to have your luggage transported each day to your next accommodation Pacman Travel, Tel: 07971 400015 and other local taxi companies will provide this service.

Sunset over Curbar from Curbar Gap

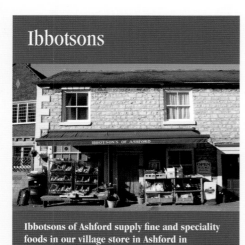

Ibbotsons

Ibbotsons of Ashford supply fine and speciality foods in our village store in Ashford in Derbyshire. As well as home made pickles, we also sell parma ham from our delicatessen and specialist confectionery.

**1 Church Street, Ashford-in-the-Water DE45 1QB
Tel. 01629 815285**

6 DAY WALK

Starting Point:	Bamford village
Walk day 1:	Bamford to Grindleford (7.65 miles)
Walk day 2:	Grindleford to Baslow (5.09 miles)
Walk day 3:	Baslow to Bakewell (5.36 miles)
Walk day 4:	Bakewell to Cressbrook (6.23 miles)
Walk day 5:	Cressbrook to Bretton (6.57 miles)
Walk day 6:	Bretton to Bamford (4.97 miles)

Overnight accommodation:

Day 1:	Grindleford
Day 2:	Baslow
Day 3:	Bakewell
Day 4:	Cressbrook
Day 5:	Bretton

7 DAY WALK

Starting Point:	Bamford
Walk day 1:	Bamford to Hathersage (4.3 miles)
Walk day 2:	Hathersage to Froggatt (4.54 miles)
Walk day 3:	Froggatt to Baslow (3.9 miles)
Walk day 4:	Baslow to Bakewell (5.36 miles)
Walk day 5:	Bakewell to Monsal Head (4.84 miles)
Walk day 6:	Monsal Head to Great Hucklow (6.4 miles)
Walk day 7:	Great Hucklow to Bamford (6.53 miles)

Overnight accommodation:

Day 1:	Hathersage
Day 2:	Froggatt
Day 3:	Baslow
Day 4:	Bakewell
Day 5:	Monsal Head
Day 6:	Great Hucklow

Ashford-in-the-Water

Sheepwash Bridge, Ashford-in-the-Water
Photo: Stephen Elliott

Distance: 1.92 miles
Approx. time: 1 hour

I love... how walking is such a great way to keep fit.

The Village

Ashford-in-the-Water is one of those picturesque villages that if you stumbled across it by accident, you would feel you had discovered a true gem. Pretty cottages, the 12th century church and the cosy pubs and cafés that welcome you through their doors – make this a quiet, peaceful holiday retreat.

About 1 ½ miles from Bakewell with the River Wye running through, one of its main attractions is the ancient sheepwash bridge – originally a medieval packhorse bridge.

A typical English cricket pitch is close to the village and a beautiful riverside path runs alongside the river up and over the meadows towards Bakewell.

The village is famous for its history of lead mining, candle making, black polished marble, known as Ashford Marble, and more recently for its well dressings.

Ashford Hall and Thornbridge Hall are both impressive residences within the village.

Brief Description

A stunning walk through meadows overlooking the Thornbridge Hall estate and passing the most beautiful, peaceful properties hidden away from the hustle and bustle of life. Joining the Monsal Trail, which leads to the old railway station, the route leaves the trail and enters the village of Great Longstone.

Ashford-in-the-Water

Ashford-in-the-Water:

The village takes its name from the original 'ford by the ash trees'. The famous and much photographed medieval Sheepwash Bridge now resides on this site. It is one of several ancient bridges which span the river here. Demonstrations of sheep-washing are still sometimes given at Sheepwash Bridge.

Above: The Church, Ashford-in-the-Water
Below: Autumn in the Village

Carl & Debbie Shaw are the third generation of their family to run this beautiful, 17th century coaching inn situated in the heart of the Peak District.

Whether you arrive to sit by the open fire in winter or play boules in the garden when the sun shines there will be a congenial welcome; real ales on draught from the award winning cellar and the Egon Ronay recommended menu to satisfy your appetite.

Bar open 12-3pm and 6-11pm (7pm on Sundays)

Lunch served 12noon-2pm Dinner served 6.30-9pm

(7pm on Sundays. No food Thursday evenings in winter)

The Bull's Head

Ashford-in-the-Water, Derbyshire DE45 1QB Tel 01629 812931

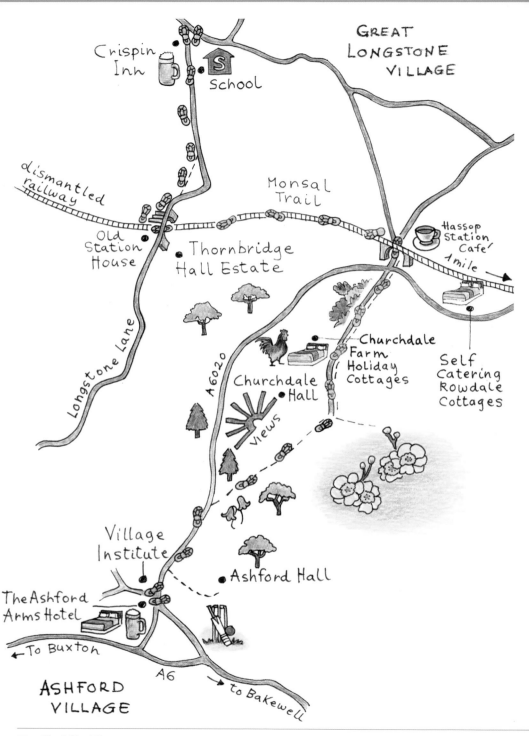

GREAT
LONGSTONE
VILLAGE

Crispin
Inn

School

dismantled
railway

Monsal
Trail

Hassop
Station
Café
1 mile

Old
Station
House

Thornbridge
Hall Estate

Churchdale
Farm
Holiday
Cottages

Self
Catering
Rowdale
Cottages

Longstone Lane

A6020

Churchdale
Hall

Views

Village
Institute

Ashford Hall

The Ashford
Arms Hotel

← To Buxton

A6

→ to Bakewell

ASHFORD
VILLAGE

Starting point: The Ashford Arms Hotel

- Standing with your back to the Ashford Arms hotel, turn right and walk to the T junction.

- Turn left at the T junction and walk carefully on the pavement. Just before you reach the sharp bend there is a footpath on the opposite side of the road.

- Cross with great care and then go through the gate and climb up through the woods. On reaching the field go over the stile and walk diagonally left ascending to the next stile.

- As you glance over to the left you will see fantastic views of the Thornbridge Hall estate. Continue across the next field diagonally to the left heading for the gate. Climb over the stile to the right side of the gate.

- Keep to the left side and walk past Churchdale Hall. Continue straight forward through the field and cross over the stile to the side of the gate. Join the lane and then turn left. Continue forward past Churchdale Lodge and Cottages.

- As you meet the junction cross the busy road with care. Walk forward under the bridge and then turn immediately left over the wall and join the path leading to the Monsal trail. Ignore the footpaths on the right and walk up a short distance to join the trail.

- Turn right on the Monsal trail and continue to walk along until you go under the bridge with the old station house on your left (now

Coco the cockapoo who did all the 35 miles

a private residence). Turn right climbing the steps up the side of the bridge.

- Turn left and walk up the road towards the village of Great Longstone. After a few yards you will notice a signpost 'public footpath' in the wall on your left. Go through and cross diagonally right towards the gate in the hedgerow. Turn left into Longstone Lane, keeping to the left hand footpath.

- Just before the 'school' sign a footpath enters the field on your left. This is "The Golden Miles" route.

Sunnylea Cottage

**Greaves Lane, Ashford-in-the-Water,
Nr Bakewell, Derbyshire DE45 1QH
Tel: 01629 815285
Mob: 07866 329691
Email: info@sunnyleacottage.co.uk**

Thornbridge Hall

Thornbridge Hall is a private stately home, a unique venue set in 100 acres in the heart of the Peak District.

The spectacularly designed Carriage House, with executive Boardroom, magnificent Ballroom, Underground bar and marble kitchen combine with 12 acres of stunning gardens to offer complete flexibility for all events from Board meetings,and bespoke conferences to Balls and Garden Parties.

For further information on Thornbridge Hall Call Jackie Morgan on 01629641006 or Visit our website www.thornbridgehall.co.uk

Addresses in Ashford-in-the-Water

Hotels / Public Houses

Ashford Arms Hotel
Church Street, Ashford-in-the-Water,
Bakewell, Derbyshire, DE45 1QB
Tel: 01629 812725
www.ashford-arms.co.uk

Riverside House Hotel
Fennel Street, Ashford-in-the-Water,
Bakewell, Derbyshire, DE45 1QF
Tel: 01629 814275
www.riversidehousehotel.co.uk

Bulls Head
Church Street, Ashford-in-the-Water,
Bakewell, Derbyshire, DE45 1QB
Tel: 01629 812931

Bed and Breakfast

River Cottage
The Dukes Drive,
Ashford-in-the-Water, Derbyshire,
DE45 1QP
Tel: 01629 813327
www.rivercottageashford.co.uk

Chy-an-Dour
Vicarage Lane, Ashford-in-the-Water,
Derbyshire, DE45 1QN
Tel: 01629 813162
www.smoothhound.co.uk/hotels
chyandour.html

Dale View
Ashford Road, Bakewell, Derbyshire,
DE45 1GL
Tel: 01629 813832
www.dale-view.com

Liz Ellis
Woodland View B&B, John Bank
Lane, Ashford-in-the-Water, Bakewell,
Derbyshire, DE45 1PY
Tel: 01629 813008
www.woodlandviewbandb.co.uk

Food/Shop

Ibbotsons of Ashford
1 Church Street, Bakewell, Derbyshire,

DE45 1QB
Tel: 01629 812528
www.homemadepickles.co.uk

Self Catering

The Smithy
Ashford-in-the-Water, Peak Cottages,
Strawberry Lee Lane, Totley Bents,
Sheffield, S17 3BA
Sleeps 2
Tel: 01142 620777
www.peakcottages.com

The Garden Cottage
Ashford-in-the-Water, c/o Kate
Middleton, The Old Elms,
Vicarage Lane, DE45 1QM
Sleeps 2
Tel: 07725 022727
www.gardencottageashford.co.uk

End Cottage
Ashford-in-the-Water,
c/o Mike & Lucy Wright,
Stancil House, Barn Furlong,
Great Longstone, near Bakewell,
Derbyshire, DE45 1TR
Sleeps 2
Tel: 01629 640136
www.endcottage.co.uk

Cornbrook House
4 Cornbrook, The Dukes Drive,
Ashford-in-the-Water, Bakewell,
Derbyshire, DE45 1QQ
Sleeps 6
Tel: 07931 787751
www.cornbrookhouse.co.uk

Corner Cottage
10 Court Lane, Bakewell, Derbyshire,
DE45 1QG
Sleeps 6
Tel: 07788 467469
www.littlegemcottages.co.uk

Orchard House/Orchard Cottage
Greaves Lane, Ashford-in-the-Water,
Derbyshire, DE45

Sleeps 6 / Sleeps 2
Tel: 01629 812895
www.orchard-house.org

Blackswan Cottage
Gritstone House, Ashford-in-the-Water,
DE45 1QH
Sleeps 4
Tel: 01629 815126
www.blackswancottage.com

Nannypeggy's Cottage
Ros McGoverne, Willow Croft,
Station Road, Great Longstone,
Bakewell, DE45 1TS
Sleeps 2
Tel: 01629 640576
www.nannypeggyscottage.co.uk

Sunnylea
Greaves Lane, Ashford-in-the-Water,
Derbyshire, DE45 1QH
Sleeps 4
Tel: 01629 815285
www.sunnyleacottage.co.uk

Foxglove Cottage
Ashford-in-the-Water, Derbyshire,
DE45 1QF
Sleeps 5
Tel: 07833 259155
www.gooseberryfarmcottages.co.uk

Cliff End Cottage
c/o Ms J Palfreyman, 22 Storrs Road,
Brampton, Chesterfield, S40 3PZ
Sleeps 4
Tel: 01246 568355
www.visitpeakdistrict.com

Tea Rooms
Aisseford Tearooms, Church Street,
Ashford-in-the-Water, Bakewell,
Derbyshire, DE45 1QB
Tel: 01629 812773
www.ashfordtearooms.co.uk

Above: Great Longstone village centre and Right: Great Longstone Church

Distance: *0.7 miles*
Approx. time: *20 mins*

I love... chattering about anything and everything from last night's Coronation Street to special memories in your life.

The Village

Beneath Longstone Edge – a 5-mile ridge, lies the pretty limestone village of Great Longstone.

Full of fine period buildings, smaller country houses, cottages, and recent newer properties which have expanded the village, the location of this village is great for exploring the stunning surrounding countryside.

In 1860, Great Longstone was on the London-Midland railway and the pretty woodland station was the last stop before crossing the Monsal viaduct.

This now has become the 8½ mile Monsal Trail, extremely popular with walkers, horse-riders and cyclists. The closed off tunnels on the Monsal Trail are due to open in 2011 for cycling from Bakewell to Buxton. Lead mining was a significant industry of the village, together with a stocking industry set up by Flemish weavers.

A church, village green, school, hall and 2 pubs are within the village and The Crispin Inn was named after its shoe industry – Crispin being the Patron Saint of Cobblers.

Brief Description

Again a gentle walk through cattle filled fields with buttercups and green meadows surrounding you.

Great Food
Great Longstone

WHITE LION

A warm welcome awaits from Libby and Greg Robinson

Imaginatively presented pub food served in the heart of an unspoilt Peak District village

WHITE LION

Main Street, Great Longstone,
Bakewell DE45 1TA
Tel: 01629 640252
www.whiteliongreatlongstone.co.uk

The White Lion in Great Longstone near Bakewell in Derbyshire is now in the loving care and attention of Libby and Greg Robinson who took over the well-known hostelry in late 2009.

Following an interior refurbishment, this popular Peak District gastro pub now offers chef-prepared, imaginatively presented pub food served seven days a week, in stylish, relaxed surroundings.

Using locally sourced produce wherever possible, chef Greg produces a monthly-changing menu to delight the most discerning of dining customers.

Food service times:
Monday - Friday 12 - 3pm & 6 - 9pm | Saturday 12 - 9pm | Sunday 12 - 8pm

Booking advisable - tel: 01629 640252

Walkers welcome - Dog friendly snug bar

Salmon & Roast Garlic Parfait

Roast Sirloin & Yorkshire Pudding

Whole Lemon & Almond Pudding

Addresses between Ashford-in-the-Water and Great Longstone

Self Catering

Rowdale
Ashford-in-the-Water, Bakewell, Derbyshire, DE45 1NX
Group bookings available – 4 cottages sleeps 4+1, 2+1, 4/5 and 4+1
Tel: 01629 640260
www.rowdale.net

Churchdale Farm
Derwent Cottage / Dove Cottage / Wye Cottage, Ashford-in-the-Water, Bakewell, Derbyshire, DE45 1NX
Group bookings available – 3 cottages sleeps 4, 3 and 2
Tel: 01629 640269
www.churchdaleholidays.co.uk

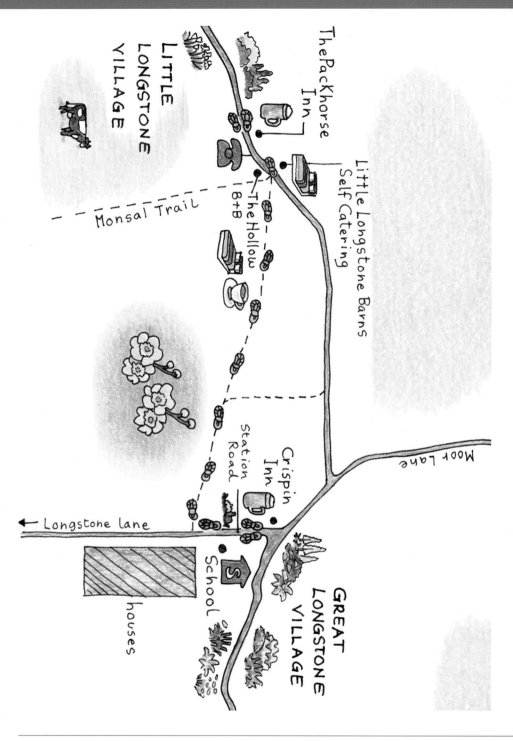

THE PACKHORSE INN

LITTLE LONGSTONE VILLAGE

Little Longstone Self Catering Barns

Monsal Trail

The Hollow B+B

Crispin Inn

Station Road

Moor Lane

← Longstone Lane

School

houses

GREAT LONGSTONE VILLAGE

Starting point: The Crispin Pub

- Standing with your back to the Crispin pub, take the road on the right hand side, Station Road, which goes up the side of the pub.
- Walk past the cottages on the right side and after a short distance

you will notice a public footpath on the right hand side. Enter this field and walk straight forward going through a gate next to the right hand wall. Cross the next field diagonally right to the next gate. Continue forward to the gate ahead, and cross the lane. Go through the stile and again cross diagonally right across the field heading for another gate. Go through this gate and after a few yards climb over the stile. Start descending diagonally right to Little Longstone.

- Go through the gate and turn left along the road until you reach the Packhorse Inn on your right.

Did you know: the church at Great Longstone contains a tribute to Dr Edward Buxton. A hero of the village, in the early 19th century he sacrificed himself to care for the villagers during an outbreak of typhus. The fever visited almost all the houses in the village, but nobody died.

Addresses in Great Longstone

Hotels / Public Houses

The Crispin
Main St, Great Longstone, Bakewell, DE45 1TZ
Tel: 01629 640252
www.thecrispin.co.uk

White Lion
Main St, Great Longstone, Bakewell, DE45 1TA
Tel: 01629 640252

Bed and Breakfast

Glebe End
Glebe Ave, Great Longstone, Bakewell, DE45 1TY
Tel: 01629 640356
www.glebend.co.uk

Willow Croft
Station Road, Great Longstone, Bakewell, DE45 1TS

Tel: 01629 640576
www.willow-croft.co.uk

The Forge House
Main Street, Great Longstone, nr Bakewell, Derbyshire, DE45 1TF
Tel: 01629 640735
www.visitpeakdistrict.com

Self-Catering

Harrow Cottage
Main Street, Great Longstone, Derbyshire, DE45 1TA
Sleeps 6
Tel: 0114 262 0777
www.peakcottages.com

Wildflower Cottage

Spring Bank, Great Longstone, Bakewell, DE45 1TH
Sleeps 4
Tel: 01246 583564
www.peak-district-holidays.co.uk

Thornbridge Manor
Thornbridge, Great Longstone, Derbyshire, DE45 1NY
Thornbridge Manor Cottage
Sleeps 2
Thornbridge Manor Lodge
Sleeps 6
Tel: 07887 722718
www.thornbridgemanor.co.uk

Attractions

Longstone Hardy Plant Nursery
Station Road, Great Longstone, Near Bakewell, DE45 1TS
Tel: 01629 640136
www.longstonehardyplants.co.uk

Little Longstone

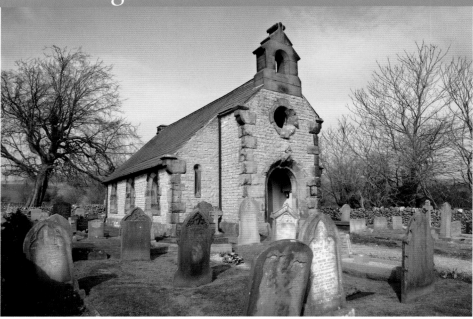

Little Longstone Chapel

Distance: 0.35 miles
Approx. time: 10 mins

I love... the sight of the red glowing, cracking, spitting open fire that welcomes you in many Derbyshire pubs.

The Village

Little Longstone is a tiny hamlet where The Packhorse Inn can be characterised as the hub of all local activity.

Situated about 3½ miles from Bakewell on a minor road between Monsal Head and Great Longstone, this cosy village lies at the foot of a bold range of hills.

The surrounding area is mostly used for grazing and the cottages are embedded in beautiful countryside.

The village comprises private homes, holiday lets, the village stocks, a chapel, the manor house and, of course, The Packhorse Inn.

This 16th century pub has a great atmosphere with fine ales, roaring fires and great food – providing a warm welcome for the frequent hikers that pass the door.

Brief Description

The smallest walking section between the villages. The walk goes up through the village passing the Olde Worlde Pub and the chapel before arriving at breathtaking Monsal Head.

Did you know:

The 17th Century Longstone Manor has been in the Longsdon family for twenty-eight generations.

Below: Water Pump, Little Longstone
Right: The Packhorse Inn

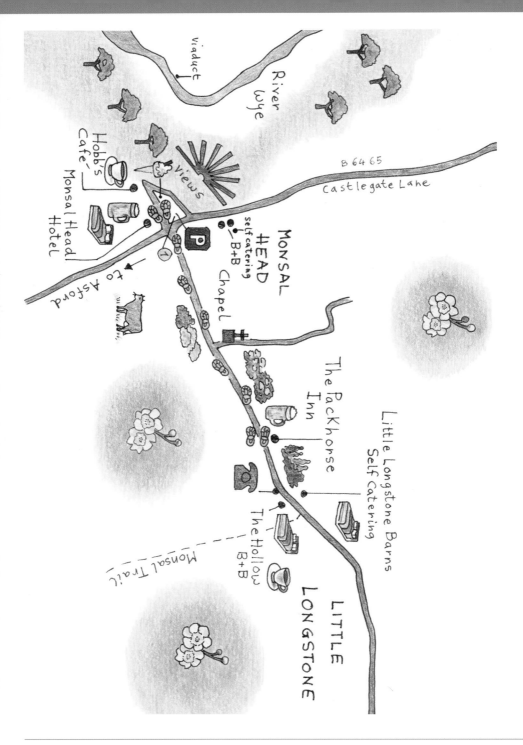

Little Longstone Barns

Little Longstone Barns provide high quality accommodation in this delightful village, right in the heart of the Peak National Park.

Visit the nearby popular market town of Bakewell, Chatsworth House and Haddon Hall or enjoy walking or fishing on the River Wye in Monsal Dale. The four barns sat alongside each other sleep two, three, five and eight people, and up to twelve people can dine together in the large barn if multiple bookings are made.

**For further details
Email: longsdon@btinternet.com or
Call: 07762 206615**

 ## Starting point: The Packhorse Inn

- Standing with your back to the pub, turn right and walk up the pavement passing the small chapel on your right.

- Continue up the road until you reach the T junction. Cross with care and turn right and then immediately left walking towards the car park with the view of the viaduct at Monsal Head.

Addresses in Little Longstone

Public House

The Packhorse Inn
Little Longstone, Bakewell,
Derbyshire, DE45 1NN
Tel: 01629 640471
www.packhorselongstone.com

Bed and Breakfast and Traditional English Tea Garden

The Hollow
Little Longstone, Bakewell,
Derbyshire, DE45 1NN
Tel: 01629 640746
www.simply-homemade-peakdistrict.co.uk

Self-Catering

Little Longstone Barns,
Little Longstone, Bakewell,
Derbyshire, DE45 1NN
Group bookings available
4 Barns
Sleeps 2, 3, 5 and 8
Tel : 01629 640723
www.littlelongstonebarns.co.uk

Annie & Peter Davey
The Lodge & Dove Cottage &
Chatsworth Cottage, Chestnut
House, Little Longstone, Bakewell,
Derbyshire, DE45 1NN
Group bookings available
3 cottages

Sleeps 2-6, 2-4 and 2
Tel: 01629 640542
www.longstoneholidaycottage.co.uk

Longstone Barn
Little Longstone, Bakewell,
Derbyshire, DE45 1NN
Sleeps 4-6
Tel: 01629 640459
www.longstonebarn.co.uk

Orrs Barn
Little Longstone, Peak Cottages,
Strawberry Lee Lane, Totley Bents,
Sheffield, S17 3BA
Sleeps 4
Tel: 01142 620777
www.peakcottages.com

Distance: 1.39 miles
Approx. time: 45 mins

I love... reaching the top of a hill and taking in the most fantastic views you could ever imagine!

The Village

This famous beauty spot, Monsal Head, attracts people from all over the world.

The views down the Monsal Dale and Wye Valley can only be described as outstanding.

The river winds through this steep sided, rocky valley with the viaduct and stepping-stones adding to its beauty. The viaduct was the route of the former Midland Railway and after its closure a preservation order was passed as it was considered an important feature of historic and architectural interest.

The closed off tunnels on the Monsal Trail are due to open in 2011 for cycling from Bakewell to Buxton.

A glorious selection of walks can be found in every direction. The best ice cream, a roaring fire or an Irish coffee – whatever takes your fancy, can be found. One of my favourite experiences is to sit at Monsal Head on a summer's evening to watch the impressive red sky at sunset.

Brief Description

Breathtaking, dramatic, simply the best!

The route starts by overlooking the viaduct then has a steep descent to cross the river via the viaduct, joining the Monsal Trail. The route is surrounded by the steep sided valley, and the fantastic scenery along the base of Monsal Dale.

Water-cum-Jolly is a beautiful natural rock formation, perfect for climbers and then the path takes you past Cressbrook Mill.

The panoramic view down Monsal Dale   Photo: Stephen Elliott

Did you know: The viaduct was built in 1863, despite much protest at the time. John Ruskin himself was famously a fierce critic of what he saw as the destruction of the countryside due to the advancement of the railway system.

Above: Monsal Viaduct from the Ice Cream Van
Below: Monsal Weir   Photo: Graham Dunn

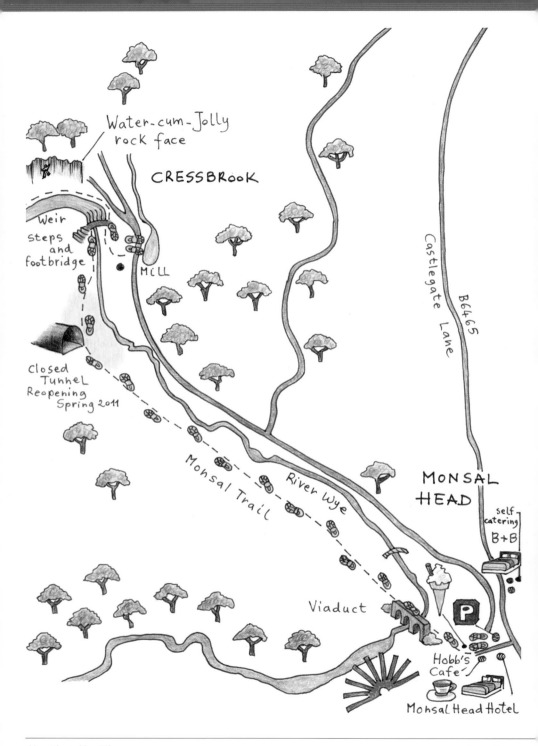

Water-cum-Jolly rock face

CRESSBROOK

Weir
steps and footbridge

Mill

Closed Tunnel Reopening Spring 2011

Monsal Trail

River Wye

Castlegate Lane

B6465

MONSAL HEAD

self catering

B + B

Viaduct

P

Hobb's Cafe

Monsal Head Hotel

Starting point: Monsal Head - The car park in front of the hotel / café overlooking the viaduct

- From the car park as the road heads downhill curving into the valley bottom, you will notice an opening in the left hand low stone wall just opposite the café. Go through it and turn right descending the valley down the shallow, short steps. A short way down turn left, sign-posted viaduct and Monsal trail, and continue downhill to the trail and turn right.

- Cross the viaduct and continue on the trail for almost a mile, following a sign for Upperdale, Cressbrook.

- Turn right through a gate just before the sealed off tunnel (Monsal Tunnels to open spring 2011, linking Bakewell to Buxton).

- The path now follows a hillside with gorgeous views of the valley. Ignore the footpath on the left and then descend a stepped path to cross a footbridge by the River Wye. Here you can see the dramatic rock formation of Water-Cum-Jolly, a great place for a photo.

- After crossing the river, bear round to the right, leaving the Monsal trail to follow metal railings round the converted mill buildings until you meet the road.

Pedal Peak District

Pedal Peak District, a project run by the Peak District National Park Authority through funding from Cycling England, has, during 2010 and 2011, been working towards the anticipated opening of 4 closed tunnels on the Monsal Trail and the promotion of cycling as both a leisure and commuting activity.

The opening of these tunnels will enable many users to use this trail along an 8 mile stretch, passing through a rich mixture of natural and industrial heritage.

To find out more about cycling opportunities in the Peak District visit www.peakdistrict.gov.uk/cycle

Pedal
PEAK DISTRICT

Addresses in Monsal Head

Public House / Accommodation

Monsal Head Hotel
Monsal Head, Nr. Bakewell,
Derbyshire, DE45 1NL
Tel: 01629 640250
www.monsalhead.com

Bed and Breakfast

Castle Cliffe
Monsal Head, Bakewell, Derbyshire,
DE45 1NL
Tel: 01629 640258
www.castle-cliffe.com

Café

Hobbs Café
Monsal Head, Nr Bakewell,
Derbyshire, DE45 1NL
Tel: 01629 640346
www.hobbsmonsalhead.co.uk

Self-Catering

Riversdale Farm
Monsal Dale
2 self-catering holiday lets
Greenhills Cottage Sleeps 4-5, and
Brackendale Cottage Sleeps 4-5
Tel: 01246 565379
www.chatsworth.org

Above: Monsal Weir Photo: Stephen Elliott

Right: Wild Garlic, Cressbrook Dale Photo: Stephen Elliott

Cressbrook

Cressbrook Dale Photo: Stephen Elliott

Distance: 1.8 miles
Approx. time: 55 mins

I love... collecting fresh laid eggs for breakfast and waking to the natural alarm clock of a cockerel.

The Village

Most of Cressbrook Dale is an unspoilt nature reserve renowned for its range of rare flowers.

Cressbrook Mill dominates this village and is surrounded by beautiful countryside with a backdrop of secluded wooded areas with Swiss style cottages in elevated locations off the beaten track. The scenery here is quite dramatic with the famous Water–cum-Jolly, a magnificent river gorge with fine limestone cliffs.

The River Wye runs through the steep sided valley – a great place for birds and wildfowl.

The original mill was constructed by Sir Richard Arkwright in 1785 and the lead miners lived in the surrounding cottages. When the mill closed in 1965, with a loss of 300 jobs, the character of the village changed. The mill was converted into exclusive apartments and many professional people purchased them as second homes or holiday lets with the consequence that the village became much quieter.

Each year this delightful village, having its own church, sub post office and a village hall, organises beautiful well dressings and a popular summer fête.

One of the stunning properties in the village is Cressbrook Hall, standing in private rural grounds. A superb building of gothic architecture, with views

Cressbrook

Cressbrook Dale Photo: Graham Dunn

down Monsal Dale. This impressive family residence offers bed and breakfast accommodation, holiday cottages and weddings. Afternoon teas are served in their newly restored orangery when not pre-booked for a private party.

This village really is a great place to relax, refresh and recharge your batteries.

Did you know: Cressbrook sits within some of the oldest active field systems in the UK.

Brief Description

The route passes the old mill – a building of elegance and climbs up out of the valley towards Wardlow. As you climb steeply, the views of Cressbrook Dale almost take your breath away.

Far Left : Early Flowering Purple Orchid
Left: Cressbrook Dale
Below: Summer Buttercups and Orchids

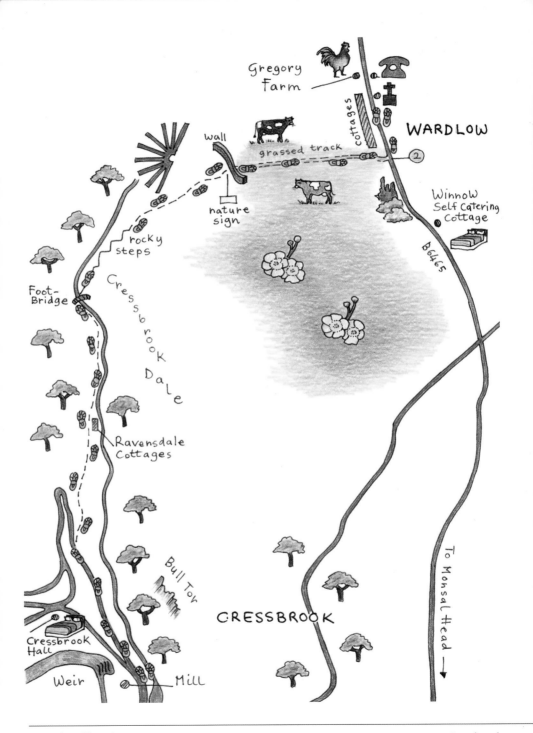

Gregory Farm

wall

grassed track

cottages

WARDLOW

nature sign

②

Winnow Self Catering Cottage

rocky steps

B6465

Foot-Bridge

Cressbrook Dale

Ravensdale Cottages

Bull Tor

To Monsal Head →

CRESSBROOK

Cressbrook Hall

Weir

Mill

Starting point: on the road in the valley bottom next to the Cressbrook mill

- Walking past the Cressbrook mill away from Monsal head after a few yards, bear right to walk up the road signed Cressbrook and Litton.
- After approximately a quarter of a mile, follow the sign on the right to 'Ravensdale – (no through road)'. Continue down the road, eventually passing some stone cottages. Follow a narrow path, keeping a fence on your right and go through a gate at the end of the path.
  Follow the main dale path through the woods and up the hill, ignoring paths off to left.

- Cross a footbridge and start to rise and at the fork of the path bear right up the hill. The path is quite steep, keep right and start to climb up away from the river. Walk up to the wall at the top of the dale and enjoy the spectacular scenery of the open expanse known as Cressbrook dale – a great place for a picnic.
- Ignore the inclination to go down the dale but follow that path up towards the wall and cross a stile next to the Nature Sign. Walk forwards along the wide grass path, go through a squeeze stile.

Continue forward until you meet the road (note: return route Short Walk No. 2 starts here). Cross with care and walk down to the left until you reach the church.

Addresses in Cressbrook

Bed & Breakfast

The Old Hay Barn
Bed and Breakfast, Cressbrook, Derbyshire, SK17 8SY
Tel: 01298 873503
www.theoldhaybarn.com

Cressbrook Hall
Cressbrook, Nr Buxton, Derbyshire, SK17 8SY
Tel: 01298 871289
www.cressbrookhall.co.uk

Self-Catering

Mill Apartment
Peak Cottages, Strawberry Lee Lane, Totley Bents, Sheffield, S17 3BA
Sleeps 2
Tel: 01142 620777
www.peakcottages.com

Cressbrook Hall
Cressbrook, Nr. Buxton, Derbyshire, SK17 8SY
8 self-catering properties - group bookings available
Tel: 01298 871289
www.cressbrookhall.co.uk

Brook Corner
c/o Wendy Morrison, Forge House, Cressbrook Mill, Derbyshire, SK17 8SY
Sleeps 4
Tel: 01298 872261
www.morrison5.co.uk

The Monsal Dale Apartment
c/o Dr and Mrs Howard,
3 Sandygate Park, Sheffield, S10 5TZ
Sleeps 4
Tel: 01142 308456
www.heritageholidayhomes.co.uk

Wardlow

Wardlow Barn at sunrise

Distance: 1.98 miles

Approx. time: 1 hour

I love... how long walks get rid of all those stressful feelings and make everything in life seem much better.

The Village

The name Wardlow means 'look out hill' and I can understand why. From Wardlow village there are vast stretches of open fields with low dry stonewalls and several hundred sheep scattered in front of you.

This is known as a linear village with cottages, farms, a church and telephone box situated along this long road.

In bygone days this area was mainly involved with farming and lead mining, which is evident as we walk "The Golden Miles" route with its humps and bumps being the legacy of the old mine shafts.

At the bottom of the hill, a short detour from "The Golden Miles" Route lies Wardlow Mires. Here you can call at The Three Stags Heads pub or The Yondermann Cafe for refreshments or if you're hiking in a large party, a luxury property, that sleeps 24, is behind the pub.

Brief Description

I would describe this section as relaxing.

Open expanses of fields and stiles stretch far and wide as you gently stroll towards the village of Foolow. Views of The Barrel Inn at Bretton (highest pub in Derbyshire) are seen on the edge.

Above: Sunset behind Wardlow Hey in the grip of winter

Photo: Adam Long

Right: The Three Stags Heads Pub

Did you know: Piped water didn't come to Wardlow until 1937, and villagers still carry out a traditional well dressing each September.

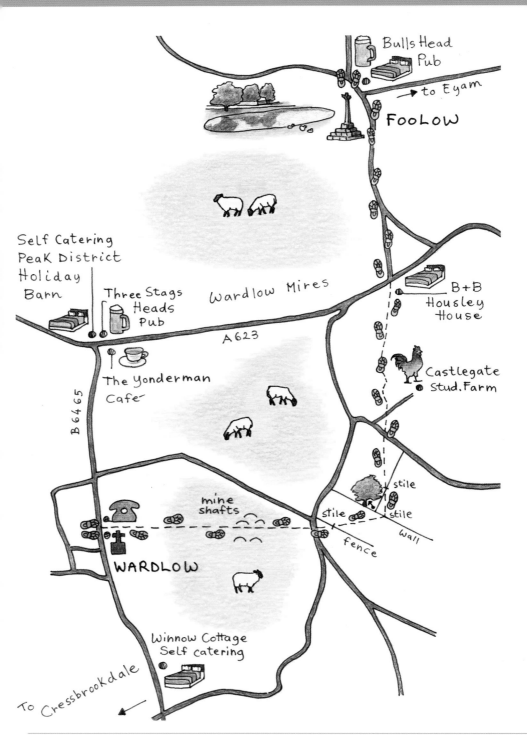

Bulls Head Pub

to Eyam

FooLow

Self Catering Peak District Holiday Barn

Three Stags Heads Pub

Wardlow Mires

A623

B+B Housley House

The Yonderman Cafe

B 6465

Castlegate Stud. Farm

stile

mine shafts

stile

stile

Wall

fence

WARDLOW

Winnow Cottage Self catering

To Cressbrookdale

Starting point: Church

- This is a difficult section because there are numerous fields which don't have significant landmarks.

- Standing facing the church, walk down the path on the left in-between the church and the old red phone box down the side of the graveyard.

- Head straight forward down the centre of this first field.

- Go through the small gate in the wall at the bottom of the field.

- Head straight forward, continue up the hill slightly to the left through the large opening in the wall.

- Walk forward with the wall on the left heading for a small gate straight ahead.

- Go through a second gate and walk ahead next to the wall on your right.

- This field is full of bumpy mineshafts (beware of twisted ankles!). Go through the small gate into the next field and continue upwards towards the gate in the left hand corner.

- Go through the gate and walk forward a few yards and climb over the stile in the wall onto the road.

Cross over and climb over the stile opposite.

- As you climb the stile into the next field and look straight forward you will see a large solitary tree (you are heading for the wall just above this) - see the map.

- Walk forward and climb the stile in the next fence.

- Head diagonally right up the field and when you get to the large tree, follow the wall for approximately half its length and you will notice the stile to climb over the wall. The path then heads downhill diagonally left to a wooden stile half the way along the lower wall. (N.B. if you glance to your right above the large farm buildings you can see the Barrel Inn at Bretton, the white pub on the horizon which is on "The Golden Miles" route). Climb the wooden stile and head diagonally right towards the stile in the right hand wall.

- Cross over the road and enter the next field, following the public footpath sign arrow to stone steps in the wall to your left.

- Cross the driveway (to the Castlegate Stud Farm) and climb

the stile.

- The path crosses diagonally right and curves around the corner of the large farm wall towards two gates in the far corner. Go through the stile in-between these gates and head forward to the opening/ stile on the stone wall. Head diagonally right and walk to the stone stile next to the gate, heading towards the large farm house and buildings. The path then crosses the field and you walk to the left of the building passing a duck pond and eventually coming out next to the main road.

- DANGER! DANGER! - this is a very fast road. Cross with care and walk along the road opposite to the junction. Turn left along the pavement until you arrive at the Bull's Head pub in the village centre.

Addresses in Wardlow

Self-Catering

Miss Jeanne Mason
Winnow Cottage, c/o White Hart Inn, Towngate, Bradwell, S33 9JX
Sleeps 6
Tel: 07971 066309
www.winnowcottage.co.uk

Addresses in Wardlow Mires

(5 minutes walk down from Wardlow off "The Golden Miles" Route)

Hotels / Public House

Three Stags Heads

Wardlow Mires, Derbyshire, SK17 8RW
Tel: 01298 872268
ONLY OPEN WEEKENDS AND BANK HOLIDAYS
www.whitebeertravels.co.uk

The Yondermann Café

Wardlow Mires Service Station, Wardlow, Buxton, Derbyshire, SK17 8RW
Tel: 01298 873056
www.peakdistrictonline.co.uk/peak-district-cafes-the-yondermann-cafe-nr-buxton/i1010.html

Peak District Holiday Barn

Wardlow Mires, Derbyshire, SK17 8RW
Sleeps 24
Tel: 07525 051226
www.peakdistrictholidaybarn.co.uk

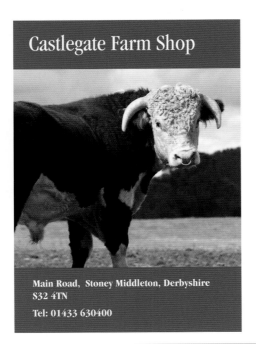

High on the Limestone Plateau, the village of Foolow catches the last light of a Summer evening. Photo: Adam Long

The Village

I just love Foolow! It's how I would describe a typically English village with its cosy Bull's Head pub, duck pond, village green, church and quaint cottages.

A medieval cross with a bullring is the centrepiece. The bullring was used to tether bulls whilst they were set upon by the villagers' dogs. This sport was called 'bull baiting', but was made illegal in 1835.

The Old Hall and Manor House overlook the village green.

This is a small village but one of the nicest places to find a relaxing, tranquil, secluded heavenly spot as an escape!

Brief Description

The Bull's Head, a quaint duck pond and several stunning, perfect cottages are all set out in front of you as you stroll up and over the stiles towards Great Hucklow.

*Distance: **1.23 miles***
*Approx. time: **40 mins***

I love... the sight of a welcoming well earned drink of whatever you fancy with condensation running down the glass.

Right: Foolow Well Dressing 2003

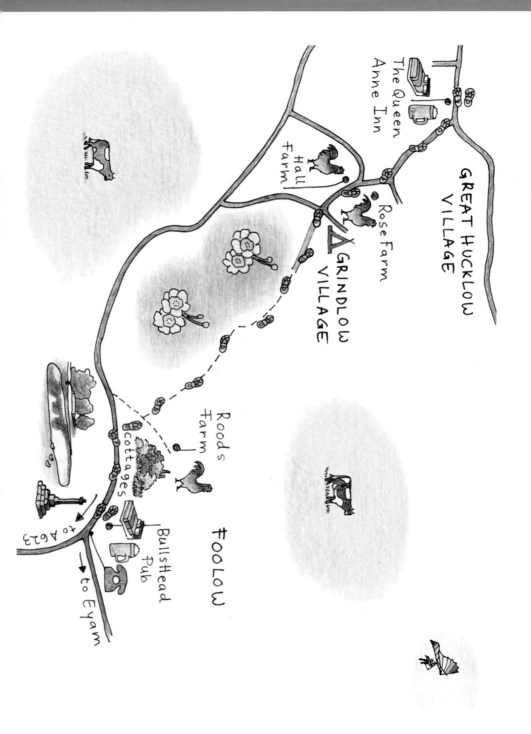

Foolow Village Panorama at 6am

 ## Starting point: The Bull's Head Inn

● At the Bull's Head Inn, walk up the village past the quaint duck pond and village green. Continue on the main street out of the village. Care must be taken as the footpath disappears and you have to walk on the road for a short distance.

● As you walk beyond the last cottage, you will notice a signpost 'footpath' in the wall on the right hand side. Cross the field diagonally left over the stile and then straight ahead passing a large house on the right.

● Keep walking forward across fields and stiles. The path then enters a grass track in-between two stone walls. Eventually this track meets

Grindlow. Follow the road straight ahead and this leads to the village of Great Hucklow.

● At the junction turn left and this road takes you through the centre of the village arriving at the Queen Anne pub on the left.

Did you know: Years ago the village pond would have provided water not only for the villagers, but for cattle and livestock as well.

Addresses in Foolow

Public House / Bed & Breakfast

The Bulls Head
Foolow, Nr Eyam, Hope Valley,
Derbyshire, S32 5QR
Tel: 01433 630873
www.thebullatfoolow.co.uk

Bed & Breakfast

Housley Cottage
Housley, Near Foolow, Hope Valley,
Derbyshire, S32 5QB
Tel: 01433 631505
www.housleycottages.co.uk

Self-Catering

Lea Cottage
Kirk Lea, Main Road, Foolow, Eyam,
Derbyshire, S32 5QR
Sleeps 2
Tel: 01433 639958
www.kirkleacottages.com

Brosterfield Cottage
c/o Brosterfield Hall, Bakewell Road,
Foolow, Eyam, Hope Valley, S32 5QB
Sleeps 2
Tel: 01433 631254
www.foolowcottages.co.uk

Fern Cottage
c/o Brosterfield Hall, Bakewell Road,
Foolow, Eyam, Hope Valley, S32 5QB
Sleeps 2
Tel: 01433 631254
www.foolowcottages.co.uk

Croft View Cottage
c/o Mrs N Carmichael, Swallow
Cottage, Foolow, Eyam, Hope Valley,
S32 5QA
Sleeps 5
Tel: 01433 630711
www.croftviewcottage.co.uk

The Old Dairy
Brosterfield Farm Peak District
Holiday Cottages, Foolow, Derbyshire,
S32 5QB
Sleeps 6
Tel: 01433 630312
www.brosterfieldfarm.co.uk

Shippon Cottage
Brosterfield Farm Peak District
Holiday Cottages, Foolow, Derbyshire,
S32 5QB
Sleeps 6
Tel: 01433 630312
www.brosterfieldfarm.co.uk
These two properties can be booked
together to sleep 12.
* new cookery school

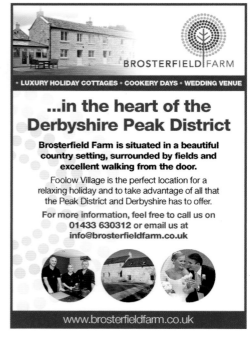

I love... the fresh air and how walking is free!!

Top: The Old Manse
Above: Great Hucklow Butter Cross

The Village

Sitting astride the boundary of the White Peak and Dark Peak, lies the quiet village of Great Hucklow.

Pretty properties line the main street through the village, which leads to the Queen Anne Pub, a cosy inn full of history and character. This used to be an old lead mining village and today fluorspar, a by-product discarded by old lead miners as waste, is extracted on a large scale and provides work for local people.

Camphill, near Hucklow Edge is home to the Derbyshire and Lancashire Gliding Club founded in 1934. From the high escarpment behind the village you can see the spectacle of gliders taking off and landing.

Brief Description

This section sounds a bit boring because I have stayed on the road that leads up to the Barrel Inn, but the truth is, it has always been a great little stretch for concentrating on your iPod and as you reach the top, the views are panoramic over the areas of Abney and Eyam.

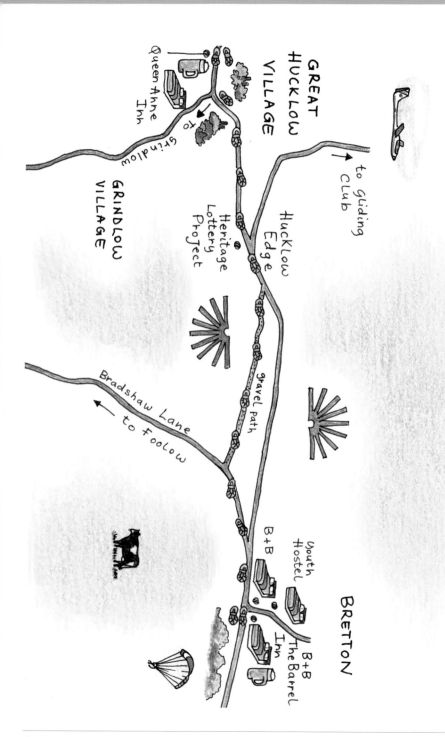

Starting point: The Queen Anne Pub

- Standing outside with your back to the pub turn right and walk back down the village and follow the road as it goes up the hill towards Bretton.

- Ignore both the road on the left to Abney gliding club and the gated path on the right. Shortly afterwards take the gravel type path on the right that cuts across the hillside under "The Edge" NB: This gravel path takes you off the road but if you wish to stay on the road, you will eventually reach the Barrel Inn.

- At the junction turn left up the road and in a short distance you will reach the Barrel Inn at Bretton.

Did you know: There is evidence of lead mining in Hucklow parish as far back at the 13th century, when the monastic grange at Grindlow was granted mining rights.

Above: The Queen Anne Pub and Gliders
Below: Village Millennium Stone

Addresses in Great Hucklow

Public House / Bed & Breakfast

The Queen Anne Inn
Main Street, Great Hucklow, Tideswell
SK17 8RF
Tel: 01298 871246
www.queenanneinn.co.uk

Bretton

Distance: **1.5 miles**
Approx. time: **45 mins**

I love... the final pub destination! Memories of myself as a child huddled with a bottle of pop and a bag of crisps.

The Village

My memory of Bretton as a child was of playing in snow deeper than you could possibly imagine.

Bretton is an isolated hamlet that lies on a gritstone ridge above the historic village of Eyam. It was the original turnpike road from Sheffield to Grindleford and Buxton and people travelled this route calling at The Barrel Inn as far back as 1597.

On a clear day you can see for 30 miles and 5 different counties. In my opinion, Bretton is home to the cosiest pub in Britain, The Barrel Inn!

Bretton used to be a thriving community with many of the workers employed in the local mines. In the 17th century, Bretton did lose some of its residents to the great plague and you can find flat little commemorative headstones in a field near the youth hostel.

Fantastic walks behind The Barrel Inn descend to Stoke Ford – a wooded wonderland that leads down to Hathersage.

"The Golden Miles" Route takes us from Bretton to Abney in a truly stunning valley tucked away in the hills.

Brief Description

Another of my favourites! The route goes down Bretton/Abney Clough, a picturesque wonderland. There is a steep descent and an equally steep climb out of the valley but persevere! - it is so pretty.

Did you know: An annual fair took place at Bretton with donkey races and a sheep roast. In the 19th century the hamlet even had its own foot race. It is said that a ram was covered with soft soap to make it slippery and the runners had to catch it as it raced along the road towards Grindleford.

Bluebell Girls on the path down to Abney

The Barrel Inn at Bretton

The Barrel, Bretton,
Near Eyam,
Hope Valley,
S32 5QD

Tel: 01433 630856
Web: www.thebarrelinn.co.uk

The Barrel Inn offers:
- A traditional country inn
- With a unique character
- Exceptional cuisine
- Open log fires

- Real ales
- Luxury accommodation
- Unique views
- A place to relax and unwind.

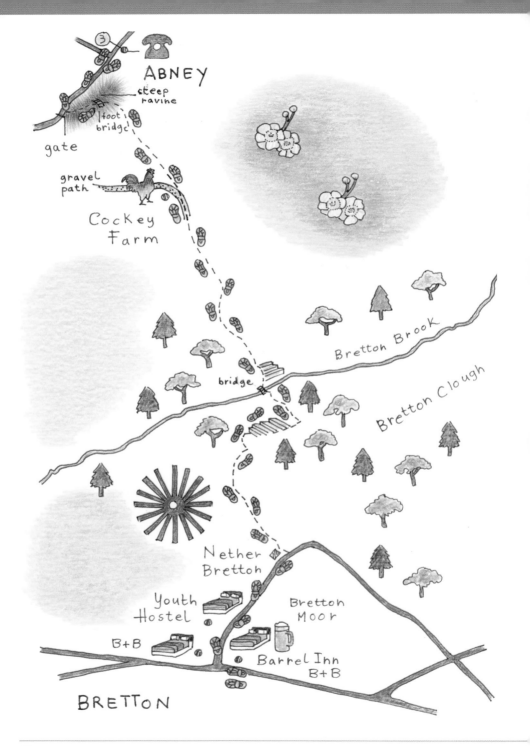

👟 Starting point: Barrel Inn

● Stand facing the Barrel Inn walk to the left of the Barrel Inn. Turn right up the lane that goes behind the Inn, passing the youth hostel and after a while you walk past a house on the left hand side.

● The path turns left here as if you are walking down the owners drive. There is a little alleyway to the right side of the house. Walk down the right side of the house and climb over the stile, entering the field. Walk diagonally to the left towards the wall in the bottom corner. Keep to the wall on the left and go over a stile.

● Go down the central ravine, only a short distance, but take care as this can be quite muddy in wet weather and then keep to the small narrow path on the right embankment until you reach a gate. Go through the gate and start to descend down the steps. After the steps, follow the well defined path downwards, the path splits, take the right hand path.

● Keep to the path with the stream on your right, and when you reach the bottom go over the bridge dedicated 'In memory of Ken Holloway'. On crossing the bridge, take the right path through the gate signposted Abney. Pass over another wooden bridge and ascend the steps as they wind up the hillside. Go over a stile and keep to the right hand wall and head for the gate.

● Walk straight ahead towards the farm buildings 'Cockey Farm'. Climb over the stile and veer right to join the gravel drive ahead towards the main farmhouse, keeping the wall on your right.

● Just past the farmhouse leave the gravel track and walk forwards down the field, towards the large farm buildings in the distance.

Keep the wall on your right and walk across the field and on the right follow the 'public footpath' sign over the stile and through the gate.

● Cross the field keeping to the left side aiming for the left side of the village of Abney and as you go over the brow of the hill, the path curves towards the gate. Enter the gate.

● Initially, the path drops down heading towards the central gully (do not follow the wide grass track to the left). This path then climbs to the left until you arrive at a gate. Go down, over the bridge and up the ravine.

● Turn right and follow the road up towards the village of Abney, where you will see a red phone box on the right hand side.

Track up to Abney in Spring

Addresses in Bretton

Public House / Bed & Breakfast

The Barrel Inn
Bretton, Near Eyam, Hope Valley,
S32 5QD
Tel: 01433 630856
www.thebarrelinn.co.uk

Youth Hostel

YHA - Bretton,
Bretton, nr Eyam, Hope Valley,
Sheffield, S32 5QD
Tel: 01629 592700
Email: brettons@yha.org.uk

Abney

Wooden Bridge, Offerton Moor

The Village

Abney is a village whose beauty I would describe as "undiscovered".

Amongst vast expanses of moorland, the small cluster of cottages and farms line the lane, protected from the high moors.

If I was a writer or poet I could imagine this would be the perfect place to live – peace and tranquility.

Having no shops, pubs or entertainment, Abney has the purple heather clad expanses of Offerton Moor, the rare and beautiful wildlife and the graceful displays from the nearby gliding club, to give you all the pleasure you need!

Brief Description

An artist's or poet's paradise – the most peaceful village of them all! The route climbs over Offerton Moor and the expanses of purple heather are stunning. The path commands views over the distant Derwent Dams and Stanage Edge and descends past Offerton Hall to the river between Shatton and Hathersage.

Distance: 3.17 miles
Approx. time:
1hr 40 mins

I love... grabbing the opportunity to do what you can whilst you can - live every day as if it's your last!

Did you know: The settlement is mentioned in the Domesday Book as "Habenai" – it probably hasn't got much bigger since then.

Right: Abney Low from Eyam Moor
Photo: Graham Dunn

Abney

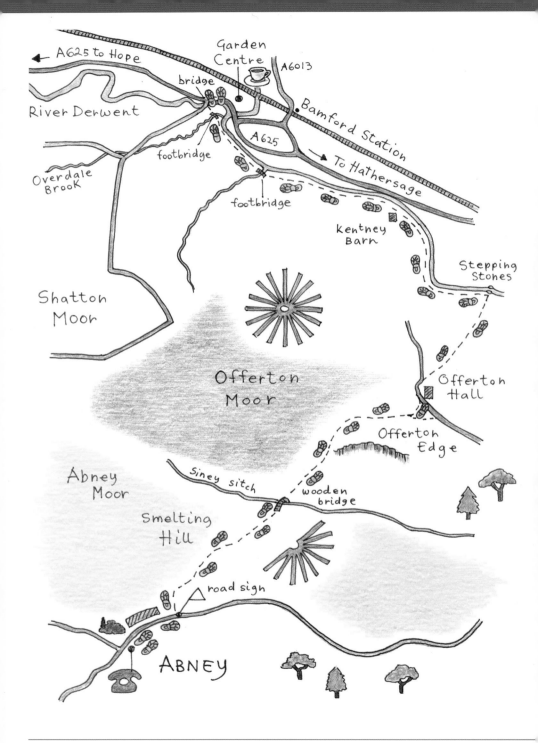

- Standing on the main road through Abney, with the red phone box on your right, walk through the village.
  There are no pubs or shops in Abney but plenty of lovely properties.

- After walking past the last buildings on the main street, you will notice a roadsign 'Abney welcomes careful drivers'.

- Climb the stone steps next to the sign on your left and walk uphill to the gate. Climb over the wall and continue uphill with the stone wall on your right.

- The path curves around the hillside with fantastic views of the Abney moors on your right.

- Continue to the top of the hill, ignoring any paths to the left or right.

- Keep to the path which crosses a flat wooden bridge over a stream.

- Follow the path as it curves to the right and then continue straight ahead until you reach the edge of Offerton Moor.

- The panoramic views almost take your breath away. In the valley lies the village of Hathersage to the right, Bamford to the left with the Ladybower reservoir in the distance. This area came to prominence when the valley was used in rehearsals for the "Dambusters" exploits during the second World War.

- Affording 360° panoramic views,

this is a perfect setting for a picnic on a blanket and allowing the sun, sky and nature to entertain you!

- The path then descends the hillside bearing to the right and it then splits – take the left hand path down to the gate/stile on the lane.

- Walk left down the lane and pass the big stone property "Offerton Hall" on your right.

- Immediately afterwards turn right down the public footpath and continue downhill through several gates until you meet the river.

- Do not cross the river at the

stepping stones but, rather, turn left and follow the riverside path signposted 'Shatton'.

- The path meanders along the side of the river through a wood,

over some foot bridges and past a derelict barn until it eventually comes out at Shatton village near the bridge at the entrance to the village.

Houses in Shatton Village

Distance: *0.3 miles*
Approx. time: *10 mins*

I love... how walking induces a great natural sleepiness at the end of the day.

Did you know: Shatton means 'farmstead in the nook of land between streams', which describes this little settlement perfectly as it sits beside the confluence of the Derwent and Noe.

The Ford in Shatton

The Village

Shatton is a sleepy hamlet in the parish of Hope.

The properties that line this long lane are absolutely beautiful, perfect for escaping the busy hustle and bustle of life, but at the same time lying very close to the excellent facilities of Hathersage and Hope.

Shatton is a perfect starting point for beautiful walks directly onto Shatton Moor, where great views can be seen of Win Hill, Mam Tor and the distant Derwent Dams.

Brief Description

Shatton village is such a pretty collection of properties that peacefully line the road, but our route goes over the bridge, leaving the village, passing the garden centre and over to the Bamford train station.

Shatton Village from Shatton Moor with Ladybower Reservoir, Bamford Edge and Bamford in the distance

Addresses in Shatton

Self-Catering

Shatton Hall Farm

Bamford, Hope Valley, S33 0BG
Group bookings available – 3 cottages
sleeps 4, 4 and 4
N.B. This is a one mile diversion off
the route
Tel: 01433 620635
www.peakfarmholidays.co.uk

The High Peak Garden Centre

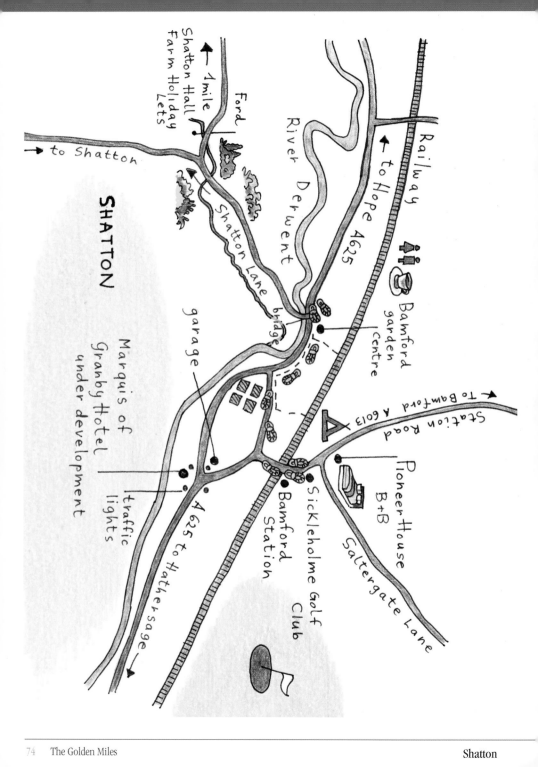

Starting point: the Bridge at the entrance to Shatton Village

NOTE: Shatton village is full of beautiful properties and occasionally some have provided bed and breakfast accommodation. There is also self-catering accommodation that offers short breaks. There are no shops/pubs within this pretty village.

- "The Golden Miles" Route passes over the bridge and meets the main road between Castleton and Hathersage. Cross over with great care. Turn right and walk past the Bamford Garden Centre.

NOTE: This is a great place to call for refreshments, a toilet stop or an opportunity to purchase supplies from the hiking shop.

A little way past the Garden Centre, cross over the bridge on the secondary footpath at the side of the bridge and immediately afterwards, on the left hand side, take the lane that cuts through to meet the main road to Bamford. At the T-junction, cross with care, turn left and walk over the bridge above the Bamford Train Station.

The Real Fudge Company

Based in Castleton, The Real Fudge Company occupies numbers 1, 2 & 3 How Lane and is located opposite Ye Olde Cheshire Cheese pub. The business consists of a traditional sweet shop and a fudge kitchen.

The shop sells a huge range of sweets which bring back memories of childhood favourites. Also available, as cordial or ready to drink, is a

selection of old fashioned drinks sold in swing-top bottles, which include Sarsaparilla, Vimto, and Dandelion & Burdock. Local honey, jams and chutneys are also on sale.

The fudge kitchen is open to the public and is where you are able to come and see our mouth watering, melt in the mouth fudge made.

If you time your visit well, you may be offered a sample of fudge straight from the pan. Samples of freshly made fudge are always available.

Traditionally cooked in Victorian brass pans to our own family recipe, we make more than eighty flavours, of which twenty-five are available in the shop. If you like fudge you will love this. If you don't normally like fudge you will be pleasantly surprised.

For all enquiries, including wholesale,

Tel: 07704 850 663 Email: therealfudgecompany@gmail.com
Contact: Monica Williams

Bamford

Bamford Edge overlooking Ladybower Reservoir
Photo: Graham Dunn

Distance: 4.3 miles
Approx. time:
2 hours 10 mins

I love... standing high up above Hathersage with Tom and my friends drinking a toast to all the children of Bluebell Wood Children's Hospice.

The Village

"The Golden Miles" Route merely skirts the lower edge of Bamford village.

Bamford is a nice village but quite modern compared to surrounding villages. Most people drive straight through heading for the nearby Derwent Dams, famous for their connection with the Dambusters in the Second World War.

The village is superbly situated below Bamford Edge and the area comes alive in the summer sunshine. Two public houses, a village green and the post office serve the community and Bamford train station is ideal for access to the area.

Sickleholme, a superb 18-hole golf course is extremely popular with golfers from all over the country, and boasts the most spectacular views over the Hope Valley.

Brief Description

The route does not go into Bamford Village itself but instead climbs up the edge of Sickleholme golf course.

For a short distance you walk along the shaded muddy lane before entering the path that gently meanders in and out of the fields, alongside the lane, to climb up to Outlane, so that you are guaranteed the fantastic views overlooking the valley.

As you near the top the dramatic views overlooking Stanage Edge sum up the beauty of the Peak District and come close to a climber's paradise. The path then descends and rises as it passes a stream and leads to Northlees. It then follows the valley through meadows towards Hathersage.

Did you know: Originally recorded as an outlying part of nearby Hathersage, the name Bamford derives from the early English "beam-ford", which literally means "wooden footbridge".

Top: Bamford Village
Photo: Adam Long

Right: Bamford Village Centre
Millennium Stone

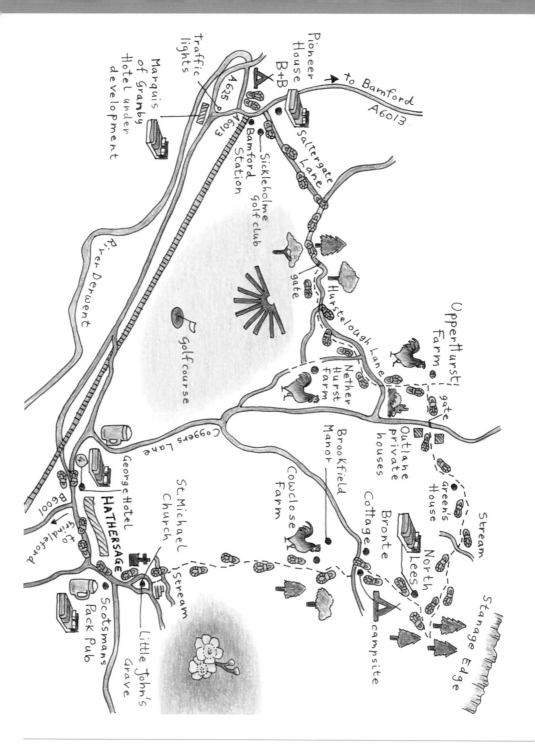

Starting point: Bamford Train Station

After walking past the train station on the road towards Bamford, turn right into Saltergate Lane.

Walk along Saltergate Lane passing Sickleholme Golf Course on the right. The lane starts to climb and after passing the second blue road sign 'No parking – passing place' you will notice a stile in the fence on the right hand side that enters the golf course.

Climb over the stile and walk uphill by the fence on the perimeter of the golf course.

When you get to the top corner you will notice a stile over to Hurstclough Lane. Climb over the stile and turn right, up the lane.

As you walk along the lane, the lane forks – take the right hand fork. This lane becomes narrow and shaded, and as it descends into the bottom becomes eroded and muddy. Just before the lane starts to climb you will notice a footpath sign on the right. Go through the gate and climb up through the trees. Walk straight ahead and follow the path up through the fields keeping to the left hand side.

[N.B. The route climbs up alongside the lane but by going in and out of the gates you get nice views].

Follow the footpath sign on the left and re-enter Hurstclough Lane.

After a few yards walk past the drive and bridleway on the right and re-enter the field through the gate on the right.

Keep to the left side of the field and pass through the gate in the corner. Walk up the field and once again pick up Hurstclough Lane near Nether Hurst driveway.

Stay on Hurstclough Lane as it climbs until just before the group of stone cottages. You will notice a stile and a footpath sign to the

left. Go over the stile and bear right up the field (with cottages on your right). Continue forwards ascending until you go over another stile at the point where you will see the farm in front of you.

Bear right, go over the stile in the fence and continue up the field. Head towards the stone stile in the wall in the top right hand corner.

Walk diagonally to the right across the field and head for the gate in the opposite corner near the stone buildings. Cross over the lane and go on the footpath opposite which goes down the driveway of the stone properties known as 'Outlane'.

Cross over the cattle grid and walk straight ahead and down into the valley.

This is one of my favourite views overlooking Stanage Edge and the green rolling hills of Derbyshire.

The lane curves to the left, walk over the cattle grid and walk past the large beautiful house.

Go through the large gate on the lane and walk on the grassed track in between the stone walls.

Go through the gate and walk diagonally right descending across the field to the stile.

Continue forward to the next stile and then enter the uneven path down into a wooded area.

Stepping stones provide a crossing over the stream – a great place to cool down in the hot English sun!

Go through the gate and climb up the valley following the well defined path. Ignore the large gate in the wall on the right that says private land, but continue up hill to the next large gate with a footpath sign.

Go through the gate and walk straight ahead following the well defined path that cuts along the

hillside towards the trees with views of Stanage Edge above.

Walk towards the gate and turn and head downhill on the well defined path towards the stone buildings, known as "North Lees".

Follow the lane down to the bottom of the drive. Turn left and walk past North Lees campsite. On the right is a footpath. Climb the steps and go over the stile. Follow the path and go through the small gate to the left hand side of the farm building. Go through another gate and keep to the path alongside the fence on your right.

You will notice Brookfield Manor in the valley on your right. Continue through the gate and field.

This part of the journey is on an incline, and can be slippery when wet, so be sure to take care.

Go through the stile and take the path that forks down to the right, gradually dropping down the valley towards the church.

Cross over the stream and climb the steps. Turn right and walk until you see the church.

Climb over the stile and turn right. Enter the church yard on the left.

Little John's grave is in front of the church porch. Standing with your back to the main porch main entrance, turn left and leave the church yard through the wooden archway.

Turn right and go down the lane, Church Bank. You will notice the Scotsman's Pack pub in front of you.

At the junction turn right and walk to the T-junction at the main road.

Turn right and walk down the main street in Hathersage to the George Hotel on the right hand side.

Addresses in Bamford

Self-Catering

Derwent View
Bamford, Derbyshire, S33 0BU
Tel: 01433 651637
Email: jamcottage@fsmail.net

Glen House
Bamford, Strawberry Lee Lane,
Totley Bents, Sheffield, S17 3BA
Sleeps 6
Tel: 01142 620777
www.peakcottages.com

Hotels / Public Houses

* Under development
**The Marquis of Granby,
Bamford**
www.marquisofgranbyhotel.co.uk

The Anglers Rest
Main Road, Bamford, Hope Valley,
S33 0DY
Tel: 01433 659415
(N.B. This is situated right at the top
of the village)

Bed and Breakfast

Pioneer House
Station Road,
Bamford-in-the-High Peak,
Hope Valley, S33 0BN
Tel: 01433 650638
www.pioneerhouse.co.uk

Attractions

The following attractions are at the
High Peak Garden Centre:

High Peak Garden Centre
Hope Road, Bamford, Hope Valley,
S33 0AL
Tel: 01433 651484
www.highpeakgardencentre.info

Baytree Coffee Shop
Hope Road, Bamford, Hope Valley,
S33 0AL
Tel: 01433 651250

Hitch n Hike
Hope Road, Bamford, Hope Valley,
Derbyshire, S33 0AH
Tel: 01433 651013
www.highpeakgardencentre.info

**Jenny Mather Artist &
Therapist**
Blackberry Barn Studio, Main Rd,
Bamford, S33 0AY
Tel: 01433 651795
bookings by prior arrangement only
www.jennymather.co.uk

Bamford Church

Swallowholme Camping & Caravan Park
Station Road, Bamford, Hope Valley S33 0BN

A small friendly site on the edge of the village of Bamford in the Peak District. A good base for both walking and visiting the local area. Riverside location with fishing rights. Situated close to Bamford Station and within easy walking distance of village amenities.

Pitches for touring caravans, motorhomes and tents. Electric hook-up available. Toilets and showers recently refurbished. Booking advisable at weekends and Bank Holidays.

For further information and bookings please call 01433 650981 or e-mail: swallowholmecamping@btconnect.com
Sorry but dogs are not allowed on site Affordable Cycle Hire also available

Hathersage Photo: Heath and Heaven, Living Art

The Village

Distance: 3.35 miles
Approx. time:
1 hours 40 mins

Overlooked by the stunning gritstone edges of Stanage, Hathersage is a spectacular Derbyshire village and the starting point for a number of enjoyable walks.

If I could bring my family to live in Derbyshire on "The Golden Miles" Route, it would have to be to Hathersage. It is truly beautiful, popular, charming and yet so unspoilt. Several shops, public houses, restaurants and hotels provide great facilities. Climbers flock to the village from all over the country, keen to explore the challenges of the nearby Stanage Edge.

The old fashioned open air Hathersage Swimming Baths provide the perfect outdoor fitness centre and it always reminds me of my childhood when as a family, our hot summer days would be spent splashing around and having fun.

In the 19th century, Hathersage actually had 5 industrial mills and although it is hard to imagine, used to be plagued by thick black choking smoke. There is a long association with the manufacture of millstones stretching for hundreds of years. Hathersage is steeped in tradition and history - Charlotte Bronte visited Hathersage in 1845 whilst writing Jane Eyre, her novel that was set in the village. Robin Hood's friend, Little John is buried in the graveyard at Hathersage church.

I love... enjoying a traditional English cream tea, making contented humming noises with my eyes shut thinking how I've earned all those delicious calories!

For me a visit to Hathersage would not be complete without experiencing the welcoming delights of the Plough Inn, near the Leadmill Bridge - just a 2 minute diversion off "The Golden Miles" Route but one not to be missed - it is how you dream a Derbyshire pub should be!

And finally the train station - great access to and from the area.

Brief Description

The route leaves from behind the Little John Pub. Be sure to glance up at the rock formation of the edges as you walk to Leadmill Bridge. The path then follows the river to climb up through the pretty woodland and then leads to the famous Grindleford Station, passing the elegant Maynard Hotel; the route takes the pavement down to the church.

Did you know: Little John's grave measures 11 feet from head to footstone. In 1784 the grave was opened, and a thigh bone 30 inches long was exhumed – making its owner over 7 feet tall.

Left:
Top: Hathersage swimming pool
Middle: Hathersage Church
and
Bottom: Little John's Grave at Hathersage Church
Right:
Top: A summer evening in climbing paradise, Stanage Edge
Left: Hathersage village centre

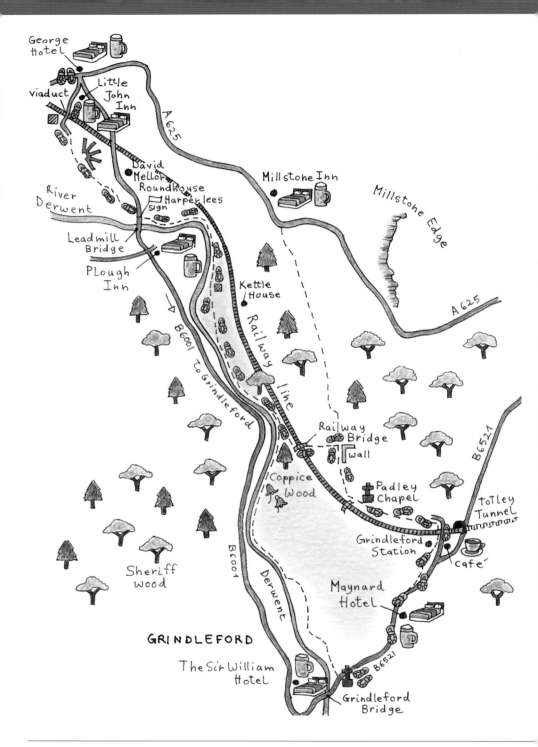

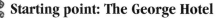

Starting point: The George Hotel

- Standing outside the George Hotel you will see the road opposite, signposted 'Grindleford'. Cross with care, and after a few yards, just before the Little John pub, turn right down Mill Lane.

- Follow the lane beside the stream and walk under the viaduct. The lane curves to the left but the footpath is on the right just next to Nether Hall. Go through the gate/stile signposted 'Leadmill Bridge'.

Walk through the field heading straight ahead, glancing to the left at the dramatic rock formation of Millstone Edge.

- Go through the stile in the wall and carefully cross over the road. NOTE: At this point there are 2 great places to visit but both are slightly off "The Golden Miles" route. A short distance to the left is the David Mellor's Cutlery Shop/Café/Restaurant. The famous round building full of beautiful gifts is close by. By turning right just over the Leadmill Bridge on the left hand side you will discover The Plough Inn, one of my favourite places to make a day in Derbyshire perfect!
Now back to the route, you will notice a sign 'Harper Lees' – public footpath.

- Follow this gravel road (alongside the river on your right). Pass over two cattle grids; ignoring yellow arrow signs to your left. Turn right before the next cattle grid and private house and go through the gate. Walk straight ahead across the field.

- The river runs on your right hand side. Go over a stile and into Coppice Wood. The path splits and you take the left – signposted 'Grindleford Station'.

- Rise up through the wood and before you reach the gate, there is a signpost 'footpath' to the left. Take care at this point because as you climb the short distance towards the gate in the wall the ground is uneven and rocky. Leave Coppice Wood and cross the Railway Bridge. Go through the gate and walk straight up the field. When the path meets the wall ahead, turn right. NOTE: The path on the left leads to the main road, and if you turn left,

in a short distance you will come across The Millstone Inn on your right hand side, a nice place for food and accommodation.

- Walk past some cottages and over a cattle grid. With Padley Chapel on the left, continue along the road as it eventually curves to the right and crosses over Grindleford Station Railway Bridge. Refreshments and toilets are available at the station café.

- Leave the station and walk up the road, on the pathway. At the

junction, cross the road with great care and turn right, walking down the road past the Maynard Hotel. NOTE: Make time to call here and enjoy the beautiful terrace overlooking the garden and valley.

- As you reach the village, walk down to the church on your left.

Addresses in Hathersage

Restaurants / Food

Coleman's Deli
The Square, Unit 5, Main Road,
Hathersage, Hope Valley, S32 1BB
Tel: 01433 650505
www.colemansdeli.co.uk

Outside Café
Main Road, Hathersage, Hope Valley,
S32 1BB
Tel: 01433 651936
www.outside.co.uk

Cintra's Café
Main Road, Hathersage, Hope Valley,
S32 1BB
Tel: 01433 651825
www.cintrastearooms.co.uk

Elliotts
Station Rd, Hathersage, Hope Valley,
S32 1DD
Tel: 01433 659911

Hathersage Swimming Pool Café
Oddfellows Road, Hathersage,
Hope Valley, S32 1DU
Tel: 01433 651159
www.highpeak.gov.uk

Millstone Inn Hotel
Sheffield Rd, Hathersage, Hope Valley,
S32 1DA
Tel: 01433 650258
Email: enquiries@millstoneinn.co.uk

Sangams Balti Restaurant & Take-away
Main Road, Hathersage, Hope Valley,
Derbyshire, S32 1BB
Tel: 01433 650665

Attractions

Hathersage Swimming Pool
Oddfellows Road, Hathersage,
Hope Valley, S32 1DU
Tel: 01433 650843
www.highpeak.gov.uk

David Mellor Cutlery Factory & Restaurant
The Round Building, Leadmill,
Hathersage, Hope Valley, S32 1BA
Tel: 01433 650220
www.davidmellordesign.com

Bed and Breakfast

Polly's B&B
Moorview Cottage, Cannonfields,
Hathersage, Hope Valley S32 1AG
Tel: 01433 650110
www.visitderbyshire.co.uk

Cannon Croft
Cannonfields, Hathersage,
Hope Valley, S32 1AG
Tel: 01433 650005
www.cannoncroftbedandbreakfast.
co.uk

Hotels / Public Houses

George Hotel
Main Road, Hathersage, Hope Valley,
S32 1BB
Tel: 01433 650436
www.george-hotel.net

Little John Hotel
Station Road, Hathersage, Hope Valley,
S32 1DD
Tel: 01433 650225
www.littlejohnhotel.co.uk

Scotsmans Pack
School Lane, Hathersage, Hope Valley,
S32 1BZ
Tel: 01433 650253
www.scotsmanspack.com

Plough Inn
Leadmill Bridge, Hathersage,
Hope Valley, S32 1BA
Tel: 01433 650319
www.theploughinn-hathersage.co.uk

Self-Catering

Morton Loft
c/o Chris Revitt, Brunel House,
Heather Lane, Hathersage, S32 1DP
Sleeps 2
Tel: 07899 796088
www.mortonloft.co.uk

Morley Cottage
c/o Mrs Janet Moss, Morley Lodge,
Main Road, Hathersage, S32 1BB
Sleeps 2
www.morley-cottage.co.uk

Sladen Lodge
Castleton Road, Hathersage, S32 1EH
Sleeps 16
Tel: 01433 650104
www.sladenlodge.co.uk

North Lees Hall
c/o Vivat Trust Holidays,
Wellbrook Manor, Garden Barn,
Peterchurch, Hereford, HR2 0SS
Sleeps 6
Tel: 0845 090 0194
www.vivat.org.uk

Youth Hostel

Hathersage YHA
Castleton Road, Hathersage, S32 1EH
Tel: 0845 371 9021
www.yha.org.uk/hathersage

Grindleford

Moonrise from Grindleford looking to Froggatt Edge
Photo: Adam Long

Distance: *1.19 miles*
Approx. time: *40 mins*

I love... Grindleford! My parents used to allow us to come out on the train and visit Padley Gorge. My mum spent her childhood years in Grindleford and it will always hold special memories.

The Village

I love Grindleford – my mum grew up here and one day my Dad drove through the village on his motorbike and stopped to buy a quarter of sherbet lemons from the village store where my mum worked, and they fell in love! Carnivals, Padley Gorge, Grindleford train station and the café all hold very special memories.

Surrounded by the lush forests of Padley Gorge, hills and moors and overlooked by the breathtaking rocks of Froggatt Edge, Grindleford is a beautiful little village.

With a great community spirit the family homes are scattered across the hillsides each with their own special view! With the River Derwent running through the valley on a frosty morning, when the mist hovers above the river, and then the sun and clear blue skies melt it away, it truly is a magical place.

Don't visit Grindleford without calling for a refreshment stop on the terrace of the Maynard Hotel overlooking the garden – you will feel you've found your paradise.

Brief Description

This part of "The Golden Miles" Route has to be one of my favourites – the paths are surrounded by greenery and the towering Froggatt Edge. Walking along the curved cobbled path through the woods, you cross a number of fields and eventually join a pathway into Froggatt.

Did you know: The railway tunnel between Sheffield and Grindleford is a feat of engineering. In 1888 work began at both ends of the tunnel and was completed five years later. When they finally met in the middle the two sets of workers were pleased to discover that their tunnels were only 4.5 inches apart laterally and 2.5 inches different in height.

Addresses in Grindleford

Self-Catering

Rylea
Grindleford, c/o Peak Cottages, Strawberry Lee Lane, Totley Bents, Sheffield, S17 3BA
Sleeps 4
Tel: 01142 620777
www.peakcottages.com

Hotels

The Maynard
Main Road, Grindleford, Derbyshire, S32 2HE
Tel: 01433 630321
www.themaynard.co.uk

Sir William Hotel
Sir William Hill, Grindleford, Derbyshire, S32 2HS
Tel: 01433 630303
www.sirwilliam.co.uk

Places to Visit

Robin Ashmore
Derwent Gallery, Main Road, Grindleford, S32 2JN
Tel: 01433 630458
www.derwentgallery.com

Café

Grindleford Café Station
Station Approach, Upper Padley, Hope Valley, S32 2JA
Tel: 01433 631011
www.derbyshire-peakdistrict.co.uk

*Top: Grindleford Church in the early Spring
Middle and below: Heavy winter in Grindleford at minus 18°C*

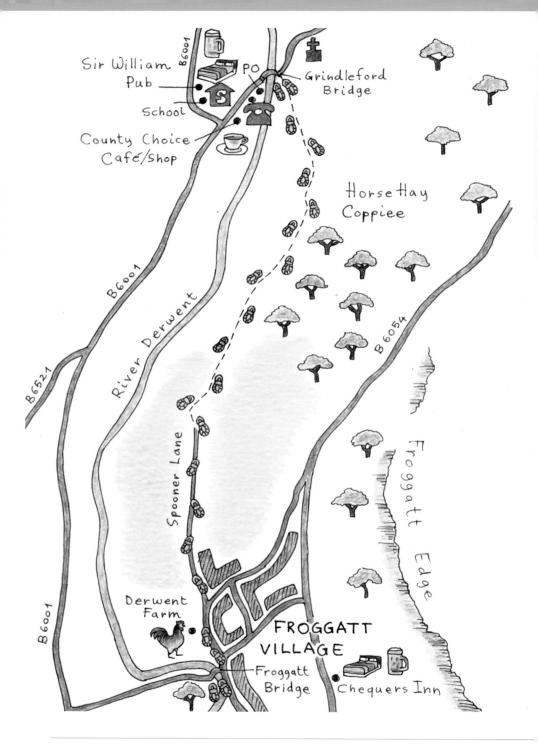

Sir William Pub

PO

Grindleford Bridge

School

County Choice Café/Shop

B6001

B6001

Horse Hay Coppiee

River Derwent

B6521

B6001

Spooner Lane

B6054

Froggatt Edge

Derwent Farm

FROGGATT VILLAGE

B6001

Froggatt Bridge

Chequers Inn

Starting point: Grindleford Church

- Head towards the bridge in front of you. Just before you get to the bridge and on the left hand side you will see a small gate and footpath signposted Froggatt, Curbar, Chatsworth and Baslow. Enter the field but DO NOT GO ON THE PATH BY RIVER! Cross diagonally over the field, glancing upwards, you will see beautiful views of Froggatt Edge.

- Cross over the beck/stream and go through the gate. Turn right and follow the path alongside the wall. Go through another gate and enter Horsehay Coppice, a small wood. The stone cobbled path leads to Froggatt Wood. Continue straight on (ignoring the footpath to the left leading to Froggatt Edge).

- As you leave the wood, go through a stile and walk straight across the field. Go through the stone gateposts and keeping the wall on your right hand side, walk straight ahead.

- Turn right diagonally and cross the field. Pick up the path sign on the corner of the stone wall. Follow the stone flagged path, which eventually joins a small road entering village of Froggatt. At the T-junction turn right, Hollowgate, and walk along until you arrive at the bridge.

The famous Grindleford Station Café

Froggatt

Distance: 1.9 miles
Approx. time: 40 mins

I love... grabbing the opportunity to forget the housework and when the sun is shining heading out to the beautiful hills.

Above: Froggatt Woods in the Spring
Above Right: Froggatt Wood
Photo: Stephen Elliott
Below: Bluebells in the Spring, Froggatt Woods

The Village

In the last ice age, the gritstone escarpment of Froggatt Edge was formed. Its power and beauty provide the backdrop for this beautiful charming village. The most desirable homes are scattered around the banks of the River Derwent.

With its quaint 17th century bridge and chapel, walkers and climbers are drawn to the area. Froggatt is a very peaceful village simply because unless you are actually heading for the village itself, most people drive straight past.

There are no pubs or shops in the centre of the village, but it is well worth taking a slight detour off "The Golden Miles" Route route to visit The Chequers Inn on the main road beneath Froggatt Edge. Fine food, refreshments and accommodation are always available at this most popular location.

The village comes alive on August Bank Holiday for the annual Froggatt show.

Brief Description

Froggatt village is like a picture postcard. A stunning bridge and then a woodland walk following the river, which opens into fields and beyond leading to Calver.

Froggatt Bridge Photo: Stephen Elliott

Bluebell Girls in Froggatt Wood

Did you know: The name Froggatt probably derives from the fact that there were originally 17 fresh water springs situated in the village, three of which can still be seen.

Froggatt

Froggatt Edge Photo: Stephen Elliott

 ## Starting point: Froggatt Bridge

● Walk over the bridge from Froggatt village and then turn immediately left 'public footpath Newbridge and Calver'. Follow the path along the river. The path goes through a beautiful pine forest. On leaving the wood, walk over the wooden bridge and take the left path up to Newbridge. Danger – Cross with care.

● Take the footpath straight ahead along a small road with some cottages. The path goes alongside the river on your left and then crosses diagonally to the right across the field heading to a caravan site. Walk straight ahead towards the stone buildings known as Stocking Farm and through a large gate.

● Walk past Calver Mill on your left and at the junction you will see Calver Craft Centre on your right and The Bridge Inn on your left, both available for refreshments and toilet.

Addresses in Froggatt

Hotel / Public House

The Chequers Inn
Froggatt Edge, Hope Valley,
Derbyshire, S32 3ZJ
Tel: 01433 630231
www.chequers-froggatt.com

Self-Catering

Jemima Lodge
Hollowgate Farm
Froggatt, Hope Valley
Derbyshire
Sleeps 4
Tel: 01433 631614
Tel: 07703 691591
www.letsstay.co.uk/

Calver

Calver village centre, monument and Post Office

The Village

This is a village full of charm and character, once you move away from the main road. With its ancient village cross and its close proximity to Curbar Edge, Calver nestles into the Derwent Valley.

With a mix of buildings old and new, perhaps the most famous is the Old Cotton Mill. Now luxury apartments, this was the filming location for the Colditz television series.

With several pubs/shops/cafés, a garden centre and a beautifully positioned caravan/camping site, it has plenty to entertain you.

Don't forget to call at the cosy Bridge Inn, where you will find a riverside beer garden to guarantee a welcoming atmosphere.

Brief Description

The path follows the base of the valley, following the river with the breathtaking Curbar Edge. As you enter the wood (full of bluebells in May), you come across the quiet lane that leads to Baslow.

*Distance: **2 miles***
*Approx. time: **1 hour***

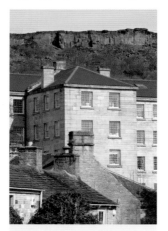

I love... the fact that we have so many beautiful places right here on our doorstep!

Above: Calver Mill with Froggatt Edge in the background

Did you know: During the Second World War lights were lit on the moors nearby to trick the German bomber pilots into thinking Sheffield lay below, and releasing their loads harmlessly onto the moors.

Calver

Sunset over the River Derwent, Calver   Photo: Graham Dunn

Addresses in Calver

Public Houses

The Bridge Inn
Calver, Derbyshire, S30 1XA
Tel: 01433 630415
www.bridgeinncalver.co.uk

The Eyre Arms
Calver Sough, Calver, Hope Valley,
Derbyshire, S32 3XH
Tel: 01433 630473
http://www.beerintheevening.com/
pubs/s/28/28569/Eyre_Arms/
Calver_Sough

Derwentwater Arms
Lowside, Calver, Hope Valley,
Derbyshire, S32 3QX
Tel: 01433 639211
www.derwentwaterarms.co.uk

Bed and Breakfast

Valley View
Smithy Knoll Road, Calver, Hope
Valley, Derbyshire, S32 3XW
Tel: 01433 631407
www.a-place-2-stay.co.uk

Self-Catering

The Old Bakehouse
High St, Calver, Hope Valley,
Derbyshire, S32 3XP
Sleeps 15
Tel: 01142 620777
www.peakcottages.com

Mr & Mrs B Finney
Barn Cottage, The Barn, Lowside,
Calver, Hope Valley, S32 3XQ
Sleeps 3
Tel: 01433 631672
www.barncottage.com

The Nurseries
Bar Road, Curbar, c/o Dr & Mrs
Howard, 3 Sandygate Park, Sheffield,
S10 5TZ
Sleeps 4
Tel: 01142 308456
www.heritageholidayhomes.co.uk

Attractions

The Derbyshire Craft Centre
Calver Bridge, Hope Valley, S32 3XA
Tel: 01433 631231
www.visitderbyshire.co.uk

**Calver Sough Nurseries &
Garden Centre**
Calver Sough, Hope Valley, Derbyshire,
S32 3XH
Tel: 01433 630692
www.iderbyshire.co.uk

Calver Mill Gallery
Calver Mill Gallery, Calver Bridge,
Hope Valley, S32 3XA
Tel: 01433 631232

Hiking Shop & Café

Outside Ltd
Baslow Rd, Calver, Derbyshire, S32
Tel: 01433 631111
www.outside.co.uk

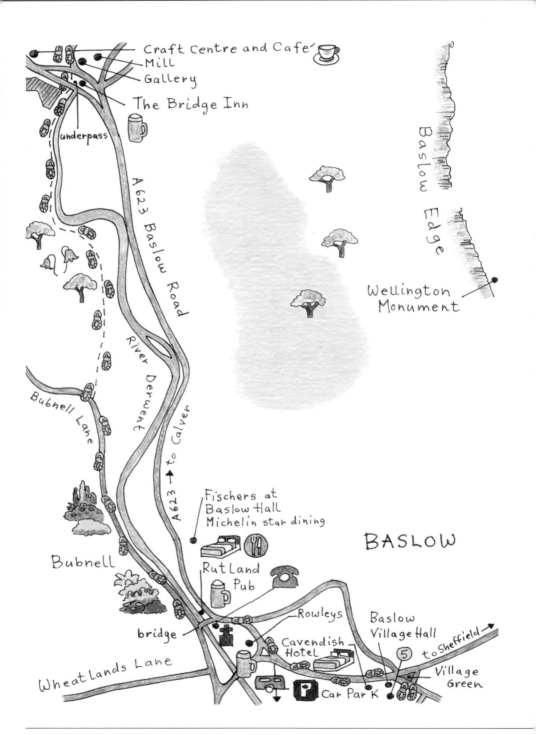

Craft Centre and Café

Mill

Gallery

The Bridge Inn

underpass

A 623 Baslow Road

River Derwent

Bubnell Lane

A623 → to Calver

Baslow Edge

Wellington Monument

Bubnell

Fischers at Baslow Hall Michelin star dining

BASLOW

Rutland Pub

bridge

Rowleys

Baslow Village Hall

to Sheffield

Cavendish Hotel

5

Village Green

Wheatlands Lane

Car Park K

Starting point: Calver Craft Centre / Café

- Cross over the road and walk straight ahead and you will see a signpost directing you towards a path, which goes under the subway. The path goes past several houses on your right and with the river on your left. Go through a small gate and keep to the well defined path alongside the river.

- Go through a small gate and enter the wood. (The path was very muddy here). On leaving the wood, continue on the path with a wall on your left and go through the gate where the path curves around to the right.

- Go through the stile and cross the field diagonally to your right heading for the large gate. Turn left at the minor road and walk towards Bubnell and Baslow. The river runs on your left and you pass several properties on your right. Eventually you will arrive at the bridge on your left, which you need to cross over, entering Baslow village.

- At the junction, turn right and walk past the church on your right. Cross over the road and at the small roundabout, follow the road as it curves to the right. At the large roundabout turn left and walk along the footpath.

- Cross over the road near the cricket pitch and caravan site entrance, and walk up the road, eventually passing the Cavendish Hotel on your right.

- Take the next road on your right heading for the Nether End car park on your right where toilets and refreshments are available.

Derwentwater Arms

Derwentwater Arms, Lowside, Calver, Hope Valley, Derbyshire, S32 3XQ

Serving fresh food, quality wines + real ale

"A great little pub with a huge reputation"

Tel 01433 639211
www.derwentwaterarms.co.uk

The Bridge Inn

You are always assured of a warm welcome

- Good food served every lunchtime 12-2pm & Tues-Sat evenings 6-8pm
- Log burning fire in the winter months
- Large riverside garden to enjoy in the summer
- Ian & Lorraine have been serving quality Ales for over 20 years
- Good Beer Guide & Cask Marque Certificate of Excellence

The pub that is still like pubs used to be
www.bridgeinncalver.co.uk
Tel: 01433 630415   S32 3XA for Sat Navs

Baslow

The Village

Baslow Village Photo: Adam Long

Baslow Village Photo: Adam Long

Distance: *1.3 miles*
Approx. time: *40 mins*

This very busy village is the gateway to the Peak District from the M1 Motorway from Sheffield and Chesterfield. Its great location makes it an ideal base for tourists.

With its beautiful church, many shops, pubs, cafés and hotels including the famous Fischers Of Baslow, it has a great community spirit. The cricket pitch and bowling club bring residents together. The village green is a great meeting place and after passing over the quaint arched bridge, and walking past the thatched cottages, within minutes you've entered the unforgettable Chatsworth Estate, through the famous 'Cannon Kissing Gate'.

Visitors can find spectacular walks in every direction from the village. One of my favourite locations is found by climbing on to the edge and standing next to the Wellington Monument – this has to be one of the finest views in the country.

I love... how walking brings your family and friends closer together.

Brief Description

Passing the thatched cottages, the village green, and through the "kissing gate" entrance our route brings us to the elegant parkland of the Chatsworth Estate, the home of The Duke and Duchess of Devonshire, into a world where time appears to have stood still for hundreds of years!.

Baslow Edge   Photo: Graham Dunn

Did you know: The bridge over the River Derwent was built in the 17th century and features a toll booth big enough for a single person. This bridge is the only one crossing the Derwent to have remained undestroyed by floods.

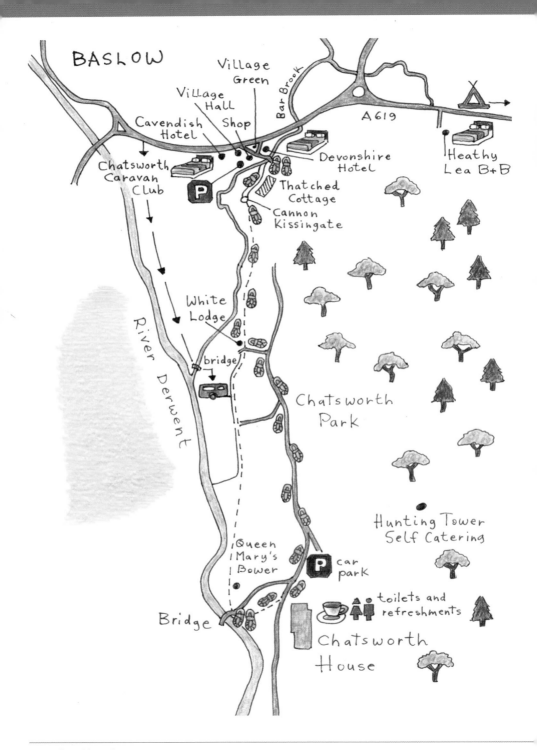

BASLOW

Village Green

Village Hall

Cavendish Hotel

Shop

Bar Brook

A619

Devonshire Hotel

Heathy Lea B+B

Chatsworth Caravan Club

Thatched Cottage

Cannon Kissingate

White Lodge

bridge

Chatsworth Park

River Derwent

Hunting Tower Self Catering

Queen Mary's Bower

car park

Bridge

toilets and refreshments

Chatsworth House

Starting point: Baslow Car Park

- As you leave the car park turn to your right.
- Walk over the small bridge and turn immediately right on to the path, signposted Chatsworth.
- Keep walking until you enter into Chatsworth Park through the Cannon Kissing Gate. This is a special gate that allows wheelchair access to the estate.
- Take the path straight ahead and keep walking until you reach the White Lodge.
- Turn left and when you meet the junction turn right.
- Head towards Chatsworth House and where the road forks, take the lower road.

- Toilets and refreshments are available here at Chatsworth House.
- As you cross the car park, keeping the wall of Chatsworth House on your left, take the path over the grass towards the bridge (see map).

Rowley's

After a morning walk around Derbyshire why not visit Rowley's Restaurant and Bar to sample the delights of the area.

Lunch is served 12 noon until 2.30 p.m.
Monday to Saturday and 12 noon until 3.00 p.m. on Sunday.

Dinner available each evening from 6.00 p.m. (Closed Sunday Evening)

**If you wish to reserve a table please
call 01246 583880 or drop in for a warm welcome.**

Local Beers - Local Food – Local Producers

Addresses in Baslow

Restaurants

Rowley's
Church Lane, Baslow, Derbyshire,
DE45 1RY
Tel: 01246 583880
www.rowleysrestaurant.co.uk

Il Lupo Ristorante Italiano
Eaton Hill, Baslow, Bakewell,
Derbyshire, DE45 1SB
Tel: 01246 583164
www.illuporistorante.com

Cafés

Charlie's Café & Bistro
Church Street, Baslow, Derbyshire,
DE45 1RY
Tel: 01246 582619
www.peakdistrictonline.co.uk

Café on the Green
Nether End, Baslow, Bakewell,
Derbyshire, D45 1SR
Tel: 01246 583000
www.visitderbyshire.co.uk

Hotels / Public Houses

The Devonshire Arms Hotel
Nether End, Baslow, Derbyshire,
DE45 1SR
Tel: 01246 582551
www.thedevonshirebaslow.co.uk

The Cavendish Hotel
Baslow, Derbyshire, DE45 1SP
Tel: 01246 582311
www.cavendish-hotel.net

Wheatsheaf Hotel
Nether End, Baslow, Bakewell,
Derbyshire, DE45 1SR
Tel: 01246 582240
www.marstonsinns.co.uk

Fischers at Baslow Hall
Baslow Hall, Calver Rd, Baslow,
Bakewell, DE45 1RR
Tel: 01246 583259
www.fischers-baslowhall.co.uk

Rutland Arms
Calver Road, Baslow, Bakewell,
Derbyshire, DE45 1RP
Tel: 01246 582276
www.rutlandarmsbaslow.co.uk

Self-Catering

Clematis Cottage
School Lane, Baslow, Bakewell,
DE45 1RZ
Sleeps 4
Tel: 01246 582108
www.sykescottages.co.uk

Tom's Cottage
2 Church Terrace, Church Street,
Baslow, Nr Bakewell, DE45 1RY
Sleeps 6
Tel: 01246 583399
www.bakewellholidays.com

Tick Tock Cottage
Gorse Bank Lane, Baslow, DE45 1SG
Sleeps 6
Tel: 01246 582625
www.peak-district-cottages.com

Hall Cottage
c/o Peak Cottages,
Strawberry Lee Lane, Totley Bents,
Sheffield, S17 3BA
Sleeps 4
Tel: 01142 620777
www.peakcottages.com

Rossett Green
Peak Cottages, Strawberry Lee Lane,
Totley Bents, Sheffield, S17 3BA
Sleeps 5
Tel: 01142 620777
www.peakcottages.com

Bed and Breakfast

Heathy Lea (situated on the
Chatsworth Estate but accessed via
Baslow), Chesterfield Road, Baslow,
Derbyshire, DE45 1PQ
Tel: 01246 583842
www.heathylea.co.uk

Attractions

Baslow Pottery
Art & Craft Shops, Ivy House,
Nether End, Baslow DE45 1SR
Tel: 01246 583838
www.baslowpottery.co.uk

Curbar Gap

This is...

Enjoying it all at Chatsworth

Unforgettable days out and nights in

Explore the house and garden
Find fun for the whole family in the farmyard
Indulge yourself with shopping and dining delights
Make more of your visit and spend the night

DEVONSHIRE
HOTELS & RESTAURANTS

CAVENDISH
HOTEL

Book your advanced tickets now at **www.chatsworth.org**
And for more information on our range of hotels and holiday
cottages visit **www.chatsworth.org/stay-with-us**

CHATSWORTH

Chatsworth

Autumn light hits Chatsworth's golden frontage

*Distance: **0.6 miles***
*Approx. time: **20 mins***

I love... Chatsworth! My favourite place in the whole wide world! The window frames shimmer as if made of gold in the evening sunset!

The Estate

One of the most beloved, historic estates in the country, Chatsworth House attracts visitors from all over the world. The home of the Duke and Duchess of Devonshire, it is one of the finest stately homes in the United Kingdom and provides an ever changing display of antiques, artifacts and treasures collected over many centuries.

No matter how many times you visit Chatsworth House and whatever the weather, whatever the season, there is always a source of amazement!.

The famous garden is full of unusual displays of flowers and even in wet weather, watching the raindrops falling on the petals is beautiful. There is always plenty to occupy your time by exploring the farmyard, admiring the sculptures and frequenting the restaurants and shops.

Every year a wide variety of events take place – horse trials, the Chatsworth country fair and the occasional open-air concert where you can enjoy the pleasures of Chatsworth with friends and family. Chatsworth boasts a long tradition of inspirational entertaining and is delighted to cater for weddings and all manner of special events..

Check out the self-catering accommodation owned by Chatsworth, providing luxury accommodation on the estate, such as the dramatic hunting tower or the secluded paradise of Swiss Cottage on the edge of the lake, high above Chatsworth.

What I find truly special about the Chatsworth Estate is that visitors are able to stroll around the estate free of charge, surrounded by the beautiful Chatsworth deer and newborn lambs whilst soaking up the natural beauty, that makes our English countryside so special.

Brief Description

No matter how many times you visit Chatsworth, no matter whatever the weather or whatever the season, you always leave impressed and inspired by its natural beauty. The farmyard, Chatsworth House itself and the carefully manicured gardens combine to form an absolute treat. The vast expense of parkland brings you into close contact with nature at its best - the deer, lambs and the panoramic views all delight the eye!

Chatsworth in the Autumn Photo: Adam Long

Did you know:
Although the course of the river through the Chatsworth Estate looks natural – it isn't. The whole landscape has been carefully engineered to look this way, following a more formal past.

Chatsworth Photo: Graham Dunn

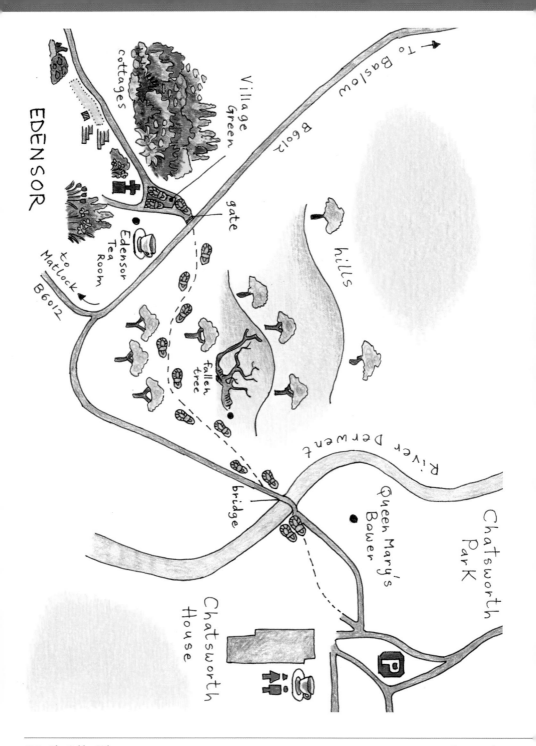

Starting point: Chatsworth Bridge

- Immediately after crossing the bridge take the main gravel path, on the right, up and over towards a large fallen tree trunk.

- As you go over the hill you get a great view of Edensor village.
- The path descends to meet the main road through the estate.

- Carefully cross and go through the gate next to the cattle grid in to the pretty village.

Addresses in Chatsworth

Attractions

Chatsworth House and Gardens
Chatsworth, Bakewell, Derbyshire,
DE45 1PP
Tel: 01246 585300
www.chatsworth.org

Chatsworth Garden Centre Ltd
Calton Lees, Beeley, Matlock,
Derbyshire, DE4 2NX
Tel: 01629 734004

Chatsworth Farmyard & Adventure Playground
Chatsworth, Bakewell, Derbyshire,
DE45 1PP
Tel: 01246 585300
www.chatsworth.org

Self-Catering

The Hunting Tower
Chatsworth, Bakewell, Derbyshire,
DE45 1PP
Sleeps 6
Tel: 01246 565379
www.chatsworth.org

Swiss Cottage
Chatsworth, Bakewell, Derbyshire,
DE45 1PP
Sleeps 6
Tel: 01246 565379
www.chatsworth.org

Heathy Lea Barn
Sleeps 4
Tel: 01246 565379
www.chatsworth.org

Stable Cottage
Sleeps 2-4
Tel: 01246 565379
www.chatsworth.org

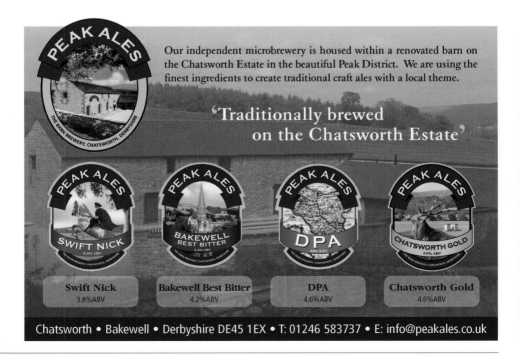

Edensor

The Estate

Edensor Village   Photo: Adam Long

Distance: 3.46 miles
Approx. time:
1 hour 45 mins

The graceful spire of the large church dominates this little village.

Edensor reminds me of one of those ideal model villages I visited as a child. Surrounded by a stone wall, the village is made up of individually designed properties from Norman to Jacobean, Swiss Style to Italian. In one of the most idyllic locations in the country, Edensor is owned by the Chatsworth Estate.

A visit to Edensor would not be complete without calling at the quaint tea room. Please note that under the current management it is not open on Mondays and Tuesdays. Also, they provide food to take away and flask refills.

On an historical note, the churchyard is the final resting place of two famous people, Joseph Paxton, who modeled and landscaped the gardens at Chatsworth and Kathleen Kennedy, the sister of John F Kennedy, the late President of the U.S.A. A number of the Dukes & Duchesses of Devonshire are also buried here.

A visit in spring is especially beautiful when the small gardens come alive with the most gorgeous displays of tulips, daffodils and every other spring flower in bud. For a special souvenir, look out for the home made jams, chutneys or preserves made by the local residents.

I love... how the 35 mile walk has brought all the best bits together and created the perfect Golden Miles.

Brief Description

This section of the walk over to Bakewell is probably one of the most stunning areas in the whole of the country. As you climb above the Chatsworth Estate there are 360° panoramic views of the surrounding countryside landscape. The route then descends through the trees to the market town of Bakewell.

Right: Aerial view of Edensor Village

Photo: Heath and Heaven, Living Art

Right: Edensor Village
Photo: Bridget Flemming

Addresses in Edensor

Attractions

The Edensor Tea Room
Chatsworth, Bakewell, Derbyshire, DE45 1PP
Tel: 01246 582283
www.derbyshire-peakdistrict.co.uk

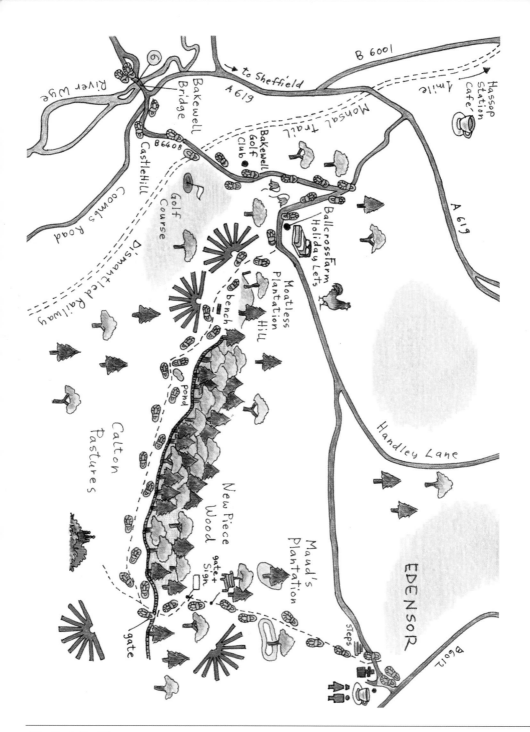

Starting point: St Peter's Church

- Facing the church, take the road to the right hand side. Walk up past the beautiful, individually designed cottages.

- After a short distance, just before the grass embankment on the left, turn left up several steep steps signposted – 'Footpath to Rowsley'. Go through the metal gate and cross diagonally right towards the wooden marker post.

- The route is heading to New Piece Wood at the top of the hill, continue straight ahead and walk in between the two dense wooded areas (which are fenced off) this area is known as Maud's Plantation. As you ascend, you do actually notice a large wooden gate in the stone wall at the top of the hill and this is the entrance to the wood you are heading for.

- As you walk in between the 2 wooded areas, take the left hand side to avoid the gully and continue up the hill.

- As you climb higher there is a bench which is a great place to rest and to enjoy the view.

- The lasting impressions of this climb are those of the stunning landscape surrounding the river Derwent and the views across the Chatsworth Estate, particularly the hunting tower, the water fountain and the deer and lambs.

- Continue to the large wooden gate and stile next to the map and information sign for Chatsworth Estate.

- Walk up through the wood on the wide path and go through the gate which opens outwards. Walk straight ahead and about halfway down the field you will notice a wooden signpost. Turn right here and walk up the centre of the field.

- Climb over the stile and as you enter the next field, ignore what appears to be the obvious route to the left but, instead, walk straight ahead up the centre of this very long field, keeping the woodland edge on your right.

- You will eventually reach a pond – a great place for a flask of coffee and a biscuit!

- Go through the gate on the left hand side of the pond, turn right and after a few yards go through another gate.

- Follow the sign to 'Ballcross' and veer right up the hillside following the visible track, this area is known as Moatless Plantation. As you approach the brow of the hill, you will come across a wooden bench overlooking the valley.

- As you curve around the hill, another bench provides a different view.

- Follow the track downwards, climb the stile next to the gate and walk along the lane to meet the road. Follow this road to the left down the hill passing Ballcross Farm and heading towards Bakewell.

- Continue on this road and as it winds down the hillside there are great views of Bakewell.

- Walk past Bakewell Golf Club, on the right, over the bridge (passing the old station below).

- At the junction turn left and walk on the pavement down the road into Bakewell.

- Refreshments and toilets are available in Bakewell but our route is through the iron gate signposted "Scots Garden".

- Take great care crossing over the road, and once you have passed the monument, head for the gate on the right hand pavement to enter Scots Garden (do not go over the bridge).

Below: Fallow Deer in the thick of Winter at Edensor

Bakewell

The first day of Spring at Bakewell Bridge

Distance: 1.87 miles
Approx. time: 50 mins

I love... just looking at the beauty of nature - the pink blossom trees and the graceful white swans on the river.

The Town

Think of Bakewell and thoughts of Bakewell market and Bakewell pudding spring to mind!

This picturesque historic market town is a much loved and visited base for many tourists to the area. It has so much to offer and entertain, whether it be feeding the ducks along the River Wye with its gothic 5 arched, 14th century bridge, or wandering around the many interesting shops, pubs, restaurants, cafés or the old museum.

Every Monday, the famous Bakewell farmers' market attracts people from far and wide. You can mingle with the crowds of local farmers whose main purpose is to buy and sell their bleating or mooing animals, whilst taking in those beautiful, magical, country scenes!

With its golf course, swimming pool, easy access to the Monsal Trail and the numerous walks from the area, you will never be stuck for something to do.

Don't forget to visit the new Bluebell Wood shop in the centre of the village for some bargain souvenirs!

Brief Description

Bakewell is the busiest town on "The Golden Miles" Route, famous for its weekly farmers' market, its annual fair and, of course, the Bakewell pudding. The route doesn't go through the town, but passes through Scots Garden by the river, next to the famous 5 arched bridge. The route then passes the old Lumford cottages and mill and after a short distance on the A6, joins a beautiful path up and over the meadows, alongside the river into Ashford In The Water.

Did you know: Bakewell's name is said to derive from the warm springs in the area - the Domesday book entry calls the town 'Badequella', meaning Bath-well.

A perfect Bakewell Summers Evening

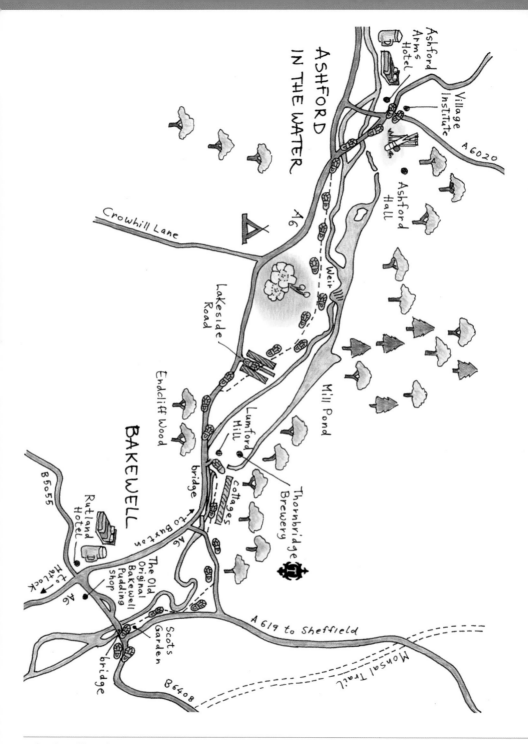

Starting point: Bakewell Bridge

- Standing on the bridge walk away from the town and take the gate on the left hand side entering into Scots Garden.

- Pass through the field, keeping the river on your left. Pass through two small gates and aim towards the gate with the signpost. As you enter the lane turn left.

- The road passes Lumford Cottages. Although a signpost says 'Strictly access only' continue straight ahead. (Trust me! – You'll be fine!)

- Eventually you will reach Lumford Mill. This is the new Thornbridge Brewery site where there is a new brewery shop open 9.00am till

4.00pm Mon to Fri and guided brewery tours available with limited spaces, so you need to call to reserve your booking. Head left and cross over the small bridge.

- Taking great care, turn right onto the main road (A6) keeping to the pavement.

- Walk along up the hill and turn right when you reach Lakeside Road.

- Walk past the houses and halfway down the road, on the left is an old lamppost. Take this narrow pathway on the left and after climbing a stile you will enter a field.

- Llamas are usually kept in this field so you are advised to stay on the marked path. Eventually you will pass a weir and the river on your right.

- The signpost says 'No access to river – Danger keep to path'.

- Initially the path goes down and then up the meadow – you should continue to follow this well-defined and well trodden path, keeping the river on your right.

- At the end of the path, head towards the gate in the wall and walk on to the main road (A6) carefully. Walk a few yards to your right and turn immediately right over the bridge.

- Follow this road and at the junction cross carefully to enter Ashford Village.

- On the left is the Ashford Arms Hotel. This is where the walk ends.

Addresses in Bakewell

Attractions

Thornbridge Brewery
Riverside Brewery, Buxton Road, Bakewell, DE45 1GS
Tel: 01629 641000
www.thornbridgebrewery.co.uk
New Brewery shop and guided brewery tours available

M & C Collection of Historic Motorcycles
Tannery House, Matlock Street, Bakewell, Derbyshire, DE45 1EE
Tel: 01629 815011
Email: jphilcrosby@yahoo.co.uk

Treeline Gallery
Dr. Vanessa Rushton, Diamond Court, Water Street, Bakewell, Derbyshire, DE45 1EW
Tel: 01629 813749
Email: treelinegallery@btconnect.com

Applebys of Bakewell (Delicatessen)
3 Rutland Buildings, Bakewell, Derbyshire, DE45 1DA
Tel: 01629 812699

Holdsworth Chocolates
Units 2a and 2b, Station Road, Bakewell, Derbyshire, DE45 1GE
Tel: 01629 813 573
www.holdsworthchocolates.co.uk

Bloomers Original Bakewell Puddings Ltd
Granby Cottage, Water Lane, Bakewell, DE45 1EU
Tel: 01629 814844

The Rutland Arms Antiques Centre
The Square, Bakewell, DE45 1BT
Tel: 01629 810468
www.therutlandarmsantiquescentre.co.uk

The Old Original Bakewell Pudding Shop
The Square, Bakewell, Derbyshire, DE45 1BT
Tel: 01629 812193
www.bakewellpuddingshop.co.uk

Bakewell Swimming Pool
Unit 7C / Orme Court, Granby Road, Bakewell, Derbyshire, DE45 1ES
Tel: 01629 814205
Email: bakewellswimmingpool@derbyshiredales.gov.uk

Bakewell Agricultural & Horticultural Society Ltd
The Showground, Coombes Rd, Bakewell, Derbyshire, DE45 1AQ
Tel: 01629 812736
www.bakewellshow.org

The Old House Museum
Cunningham Place, Bakewell, Derbyshire, DE45 1DD
Ms Anita Spencer
Tel: 01629 813642
www.oldhousemuseum.org.uk

Jewellers
(specialising in Blue John jewellery)

C W Sellors
5 Royal Oak Place, Matlock St, Bakewell, Derbyshire, DE45 1HD
Tel: 01629 812155
www.cwsellors.com

The Original Farmers' Market Shop Ltd
3 Market Street, Bakewell, DE45 1HG
Tel: 01629 815814
www.thefarmersmarketshop.co.uk

The Ridgeway Gallery
The Old Tavern, Rutland Square, Bakewell, Derbyshire, DE45 1BT
Tel: 01629 814596
www.theridgewaygallery.co.uk

Bluebell Wood Children's Hospice Shop
5 King Street, Bakewell, DE45 1DZ
Tel: 01629 814086
If you wish to support the children's hospice, make sure you visit the Bluebell Wood Charity Shop which is full of great souvenirs

Bed and Breakfast

Westmorland House
Park Road, Bakewell, Derbyshire, DE45 1AX
Tel: 01629 812932
www.westmorlandhouse.co.uk

Castle Hill Farm House
Baslow Road, Bakewell, Derbyshire, DE45 1AA,
Tel: 01629 813168
www.castlehillfarmhouse.co.uk

The Haven
Haddon Road, Bakewell, Derbyshire, DE45 1AW
Tel: 01629 812113
www.visitbakewell.com

Meadow View
Coombs Road, Bakewell, DE45 1AQ,
Tel: 01629 812961
www.meadowviewbakewell.co.uk

Melbourne House
Marie Peters, Buxton Road, Bakewell, DE45 1DA
Tel: 01629 815357
www.bakewell-accommodation.co.uk

Easthorpe
Marie Peters, Buxton Road, Bakewell, Derbyshire, DE45 1DA
Tel: 01629 815357
www.bakewell-accommodation.co.uk

The Garden Room
Mr & Mrs T Sargent, 1 Park Road, Bakewell, Derbyshire, DE45 1AX
Tel: 01629 814299
www.smoothhound.co.uk/hotels/thegarden.html

Avenue House
The Avenue, Bakewell, Derbyshire,
DE45 1EQ
Tel: 01629 812467
www.bakewell-bed-breakfast.co.uk

Croft Cottages
Pat and Des Weatherley, Coombs
Road, Bakewell, Derbyshire, DE45 1AQ
Tel: 01629 814101
www.peakdistrictonline.co.uk

Bourne House
Susan Atkinson, The Park,
Haddon Road, Bakewell, Derbyshire,
DE45 1ET
Tel: 01629 813274
www.bournehousebakewell.co.uk

Hotels / Public Houses

The Rutland Arms Hotel
The Square, Bakewell, Derbyshire,
DE45 1BT
Tel: 01629 812812
www.rutlandarmsbakewell.co.uk

Castle Inn
Castle Street, Bakewell, DE45 1DW
Tel: 01629 812103

Manners Hotel
Haddon Road, Bakewell, Derbyshire,
DE45 1EP
Tel: 01629 812756
www.peakdistrictonline.co.uk

Red Lion Inn
The Square, Bakewell, Derbyshire,
DE45 1BT
Tel: 01629 812054
www.redlionbakewell.co.uk

The Peacock Pub
Bridge Street, Bakewell, Derbyshire,
DE45 1DS
Tel: 01629 813635
www.peacockbakewell.com

The Queens Arms
Bridge Street, Bakewell, DE45 1DS
Tel: 01629 814586
www.peakdistrictonline.co.uk

The Wheatsheaf
Bridge Street, Bakewell, DE45 1DS
Tel: 01629 812985
www.wheatsheafbakewell.co.uk

Restaurants

Max's Indian Restuarant
Bridge Street, Bakewell, DE45 1DS
Tel: 01629 814336

Riccis Italian Café
10 Water Street, Bakewell, DE45 1EW
Tel: 01629 810035
www.riccisbakewell.co.uk

Felicini
Marble Works, Coombs Road,
Bakewell, DE45 1AQ
Tel: 01629 813813
www.felicini.co.uk

Piedaniel's Restaurant
Bath St, Bakewell, Derbyshire,
DE45 1BX
Tel: 01629 812687
www.piedaniels-restaurant.com

H's Cafe and Wine Bar
Wye House, Water Street, Bakewell,
DE45 1EW
Tel: 01629 815107
www.postapudding.com/hswinebar.
html

Borivli Fine Indian Restaurant
4 Portland Square, Bakewell,
Derbyshire, DE45 1HA
Tel: 01629 815489

Le Mistral Bistro and Wine Shop
Bridge Street, Bakewell, DE45 1DS
Tel: 01629 810077
www.lemistral.co.uk

Youth Hostel

YHA - Bakewell
Bakewell, Derbyshire, DE45 1DN
Tel: 0870 770 5682
www.yha.org.uk

Self-Catering

Braeside
Church Street, Bakewell, DE45 1FD
Sleeps 6
Tel: 01142 620777
www.peakcottages.com

Brew House
Off Buxton Road, Bakewell, DE45
Sleeps 6/7
Tel: 01246 583399
www.bakewellholidays.com

Peak Cottage
Monyash Rd, Bakewell, Derbyshire,
DE45
Sleeps 4/5
Tel: 01142 491066
www.peak-holidaycottage.co.uk

Gingerbread Cottage
Bakewell, c/o Peak Cottages,
Strawberry Lee Lane, Totley Bents,
Sheffield, S17 3BA
Sleeps 4
Tel: 01142 620777
www.peakcottages.com

Mill View
Bakewell, c/o Peak Cottages,
Strawberry Lee Lane, Totley Bents,
Sheffield, S17 3BA
Sleeps 3
Tel: 01142 620777
www.peakcottages.com

Ball Cross Farm
Chatsworth Estate, Bakewell,
Derbyshire
3 cottages each sleep 2+2
Tel: 01629 815215
www.ballcrossfarm.com
Note: This is on the route between
Edensor and Bakewell

Barn Cottage
c/o John & Moira Beach,
Long Meadow Cottage, Coombs Road,
Bakewell, Derbyshire, DE45 1AQ
Sleeps 2
Tel: 01629 810337
www.barncottagebakewell.co.uk

Addresses in Bakewell (Continued)

Chalice Cottage
Church Alley, Bakewell, Derbyshire,
DE45 1FF
Sleeps 3
Tel: 01142 620777
www.peakcottages.com

Anne Cottage
Yeld Road, Bakewell, Derbyshire,
DE45 1FJ
Sleeps 4
Tel: 01246 583399
www.bakewellholidays.com

Bakewell Holiday Apartments
Bagshaw Hall, Bagshaw Hill,
Bakewell, Derbyshire, DE45 1DL
Tel: 01629 810333
Group bookings available – range of
suites/apartments. Sleeps 2 - 6
www.bakewellholidayapartments.com

Baytree Cottage
8 Holme Lane, Bakewell, DE45 1GG
Sleeps 6
Tel: 01614 837117
www.peak-district-cottage.co.uk

Butts Cottage
Butts View, Bakewell, Derbyshire,
DE45 1EB
Sleeps 4
Tel: 01246 583399
www.bakewellholidays.com

Café/Food Outlets

The Coffee Shop and Thorntons
Matlock Street, Bakewell, Derbyshire,
DE45 1EE
Tel: 01629 810558
www.thecoffeeshopbakewell.com

Bakewell Traditional Fish & Chips
5 Water Street, Bakewell, DE45 1EW

The Bakewell Tart Shop and Coffee House
Matlock Street, Bakewell, DE45 1EE
Tel: 01629 814692
www.bakewelltartshop.co.uk

Byways
Water Lane, Bakewell, Derbyshire,
DE45 1EU
Tel: 01629 812807

Farm Shops

New Close Farm Shop
Granby Croft, Granby Road, Bakewell,
DE45 1ES
Tel: 01629 813121
www.newclosefarm.com

Critchlows Farm Shop
Bridge St, Bakewell, DE45 1DS
Tel: 01629 812010

Chatsworth Butchery
The Square, Bakewell, Derbyshire,
DE45 1BT
Tel: 01629 812165
www.chatsworth.org

The six shorter walks

I have divided the route into 6 shorter walks for those who would like to enjoy only a part of "The Golden Miles" route or who wish to book one holiday accommodation for the duration of their stay and use their car to drive to the starting points of the 6 shorter walks.

1. Ashford-in-the-Water
2. Little Longstone
3. Foolow
4. Shatton
5. Grindleford
6. Chatsworth

See page 17 for the Full Shorter Walks Route Map

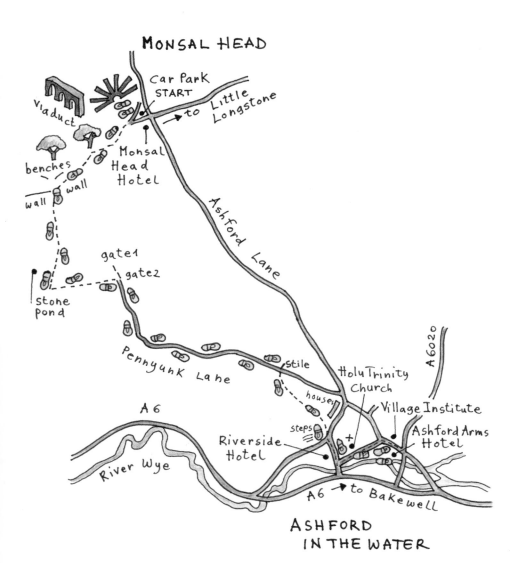

MONSAL HEAD

Car Park
START

to Little
Longstone

Viaduct

benches

wall   wall

wall

Monsal
Head
Hotel

Ashford Lane

gate1

gate2

stone
pond

Pennyunk Lane

stile

houses

Holy Trinity
Church

Village Institute

A6020

A6

Riverside
Hotel

steps

Ashford Arms
Hotel

River Wye

A6 → to Bakewell

ASHFORD
IN THE WATER

Ashford-in-the-Water
Great Longstone
Little Longstone
Monsal Head
Ashford-in-the-Water

Distance: 5.2 miles

Starting Point: Ashford Arms Hotel, Ashford-in-the-Water

Follow route directions for:

Ashford-in-the-Water: Page 28
Great Longstone: Page 34
Little Longstone :   Page 38

... until you reach the car park at Monsal Head. **The return route is shown below.**

As you leave the car park, head downhill a few yards to the opening in the low stone wall.

Turn left, signposted 'Ashford and Monsal Dale'.

After a few yards, veer left on the uphill path signposted 'Ashford'.

The path runs alongside the wall on your left.

Continue to climb with the lovely views on your right of the Monsal Dale until you reach 2 wooden benches.

Veer left here following the signpost 'Ashford'.

Continue straight ahead through a number of gates following the waymarked path.

Shortly after passing a large stone pond, turn left through the gate and head downhill.

Take the right hand gate and continue down hill.

Ignore the left hand waymarked path and continue straight ahead.

You will eventually meet a gravel lane and after a while you will notice a gate on the right, with a stile just after it on your right, which heads towards Ashford.

Head downhill diagonally crossing the field, passing a waymarked post.

Climb the stile in the corner of the wall next to a row of houses.

Continue downhill on a narrow path in-between the fence and wall.

Climb down the stone steps until you meet the road.

Turn right and continue down the road. At the junction walk straight ahead and continue through the village passing the Riverside Hotel and Sheepwash Bridge until you reach the Ashford Arms on your right.

Monsal Dale Photo: Karen Frenkel

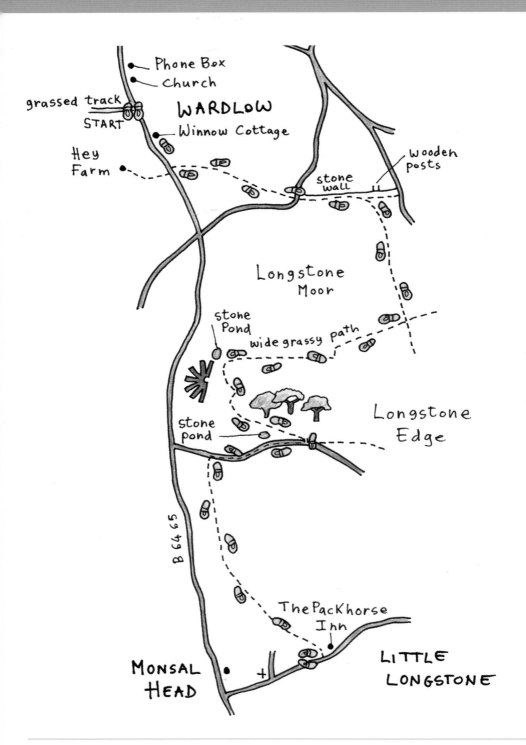

Little Longstone
Monsal Head
Cressbrook
Wardlow
Little Longstone

Distance: 6.8 miles

Starting Point: Packhorse Inn, Little Longstone

Follow route directions for:

... until you reach the main road in Wardlow village (see map). **The return route is shown below.**

As you meet the road, turn right and walk up the village, along the pavement passing the cottages on your left.

Shortly afterwards, before the bend in the road, take the public footpath on the left.

Walk straight ahead on the path that cuts across the embankment, crossing the field.

Go through the gate in the wall and head across the next field to a small gate.

Head uphill diagonally crossing the centre of the field to the opposite corner.

Climb the stile next to the public footpath sign and cross over the road with care.

Go through the gate and take the path straight ahead keeping the wall on your left.

After a while, you will notice two wooden posts in the wall, with a stile ahead of you. Before you get to this, look out for a well defined path veering up to the right that goes up

Wild Orchids in Cressbrook Dale
Photo: Stephen Elliott

through the moorland (Note: If you meet the road and stile ahead, you have gone too far).

Follow the direction of the footpath over moorland to the top.

At the top you will notice a wooden signpost.

Continue straight ahead down the hill until you meet the wide grassy track.

Turn right and follow this main track in the direction of Cressbrook Dale.

You will see the most magnificent views of Monsal and Cressbrook Dale.

Go through the small gate and turn left (do not go as far as the stone pond) keeping the wall on your left hand side.

Head downhill and after passing a large gate in the wall climb over the stone stile in the wall.

Turn right and head down the valley on the well defined grassed path, keeping a row of trees on your left.

Continue downhill passing a stone pond with fantastic views.

At the gate, cross over the wooden stile and join the lane.

After a few yards turn right on the lane.

After a while, as the junction of the road becomes visible ahead, you will notice a public footpath sign to 'Little Longstone' on your left.

Climb the stile and go through a small gate and then walk straight ahead across the field and downhill to the stone stile in the corner of the wall.

Continue downhill keeping the stone wall on your left, with Monsal Head in the distance.

Climb over the stone stile and walk across the field veering left and passing the stone pond on your right.

Climb over the stone stile in the wall and walk on the well defined path through the centre of the field.

Go through the gate and walk ahead, climbing the stone stile in the right hand wall.

Turn left in the field and head for the gate next to the large tree.

Walk straight ahead down the narrow gap next to the large stone barn until it meets the road next to the Packhorse Inn.

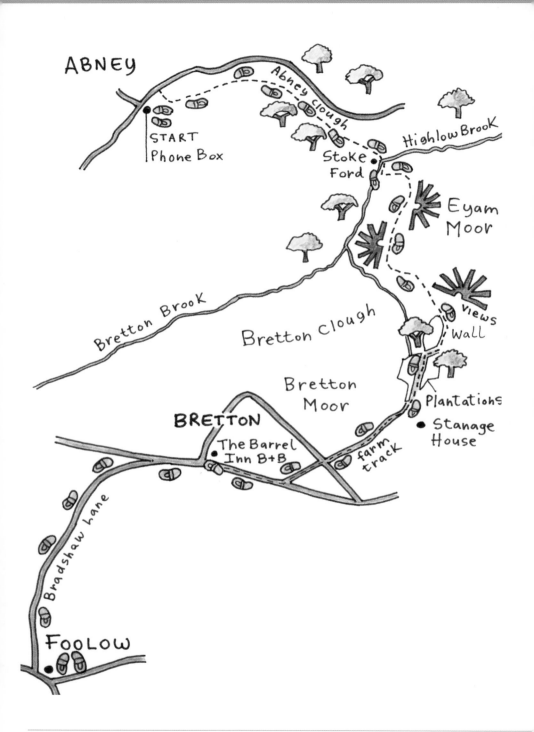

ABNEY

START
Phone Box

Abney Clough

Highlow Brook

Stoke
Ford

Eyam
Moor

views

Wall

Bretton Brook

Bretton Clough

Bretton
Moor

Plantations

Stanage
House

BRETTON

The Barrel
Inn B+B

farm
track

Bradshaw Lane

FOOLOW

Foolow
Great Hucklow
Bretton
Abney
Bretton
Foolow

Distance: 8.6 miles

Starting Point: Bulls Head, Foolow

Follow route directions for:

Foolow	Page 57
Great Hucklow	Page 61
Bretton	Page 64

... until you reach the telephone box in Abney. **The return route is shown below.**

At the phone box walk down through the village.

On the right hand side before the road rises, turn down the public footpath and walk down the lane.

This immediately turns into a grass path and then narrows and you continue gently dropping down the valley.

You will notice the stream running alongside on your right.

This first section is approximately 1 mile to Stoke Ford.

At a junction of paths with a wooden signpost, follow 'Bretton, Eyam and Hazelford'.

Go over the small wooden bridge and turn left through the gate and over a 2nd wooden bridge. This is Stoke Ford.

As the path splits take the right hand one 'By Gotherage Barn to Grindleford and Eyam'.

Ignore the immediate path that shoots back to the left and climb forwards up a short distance.

The path then splits again, take the left one up the hill and ignore the path that runs by the side of the stream.

Keep to the path on the steep ascent up through the bracken.

At this point take time to glance around at the breathtaking scenery.

You meet up with a wall, and continue upwards with the wall on your left and views of Bretton Clough on your right.

Keep climbing and the path curves around to the left with a rocky steep drop to the right.

Head for the gate in the wall ahead.

Climb over the stile and walk up the hill with the wall on your right.

After a short while, the path splits. Keep to the right hand path following the wall. This goes alongside a wood.

At the large gate climb over the stile and walk forwards through the wood for a few yards.

Follow the obvious grassy track alongside the wall.

Ignore the wooden stile on the right and walk straight ahead to the stile next to the large gate.

Walk towards the farm track, following the stone pillar sign.

At the junction with the lane climb the stile and cross over to join the bumpy grassy track straight ahead.

On meeting the main road turn right and as you go over the brow of the hill, The Barrell Inn comes into sight.

(At this point our family normally squeal with delight at this welcoming sight!)

Continue down the road past the pub and as the road forks take the left road and walk down the hill eventually arriving in Foolow Village.

Naturally Different

Sausages, pork, ham and bacon.

Delicious!   Truly local!   Award winning!

Our pork, sausages (20+ varieties!), dry cured bacon and ham are hand-produced
from our own pigs, born and reared on our family farm near Norton, Sheffield.
We use the ginger Duroc to enhance succulence and flavour of our pork.
Supplied direct to the customer and discerning restaurants.
It's so easy to order!
Simply telephone 07779 058872 or e-mail srt@mossvalleyfinemeats.co.uk
View our website for an order form and product details.

www.mossvalleyfinemeats.co.uk

MADE IN
SHEFFIELD

Lynne Wilkinson, Winner of "Best In Show"

Great Sheffield Art Show 2008 & 2009

Original Paintings, Commissions, giclée prints and cards

Web: www.lynnewilkinson.co.uk **Email:** lynnewilkinson777@yahoo.co.uk **Tel:** 07811153705

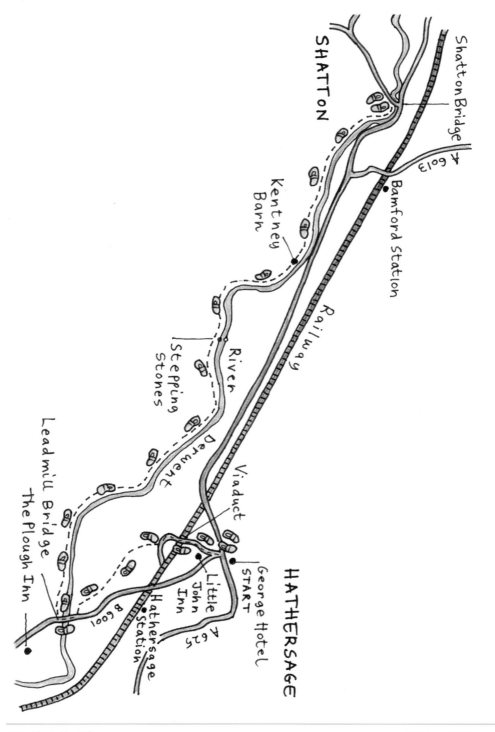

Shatton
Bamford
Hathersage
Shatton

Distance: 7.8 miles

Starting Point: The Bridge on entering Shatton Village

Follow route directions for:

... until you reach The George Hotel.
The return route is shown below.

Standing outside the George Hotel you will see the road opposite, signposted 'Grindleford'. Cross with care, and after a few yards, just before the Little John pub, turn right down Mill Lane.

Follow the lane beside the stream and walk under the viaduct. The lane curves to the left but the footpath is on the right just next to Nether Hall.

Go through the gate/stile signposted 'Leadmill Bridge'. Walk through the field heading straight ahead, glancing to the left at the dramatic rock formation of Millstone Edge.

Go through the stile in the wall. Do not cross the road but turn right and walk over the bridge (in the direction of the Plough Inn — worth a detour!) and then immediately turn right through the gate and follow the footpath sign to 'Shatton'. This is a riverside path that gently meanders along the river all the way until you eventually arrive at the bridge in Shatton.

The River Derwent snakes past the village of Bamford, Peak District
Photo: Adam Long

Hathersage on a Spring Evening
Photo: Adam Long

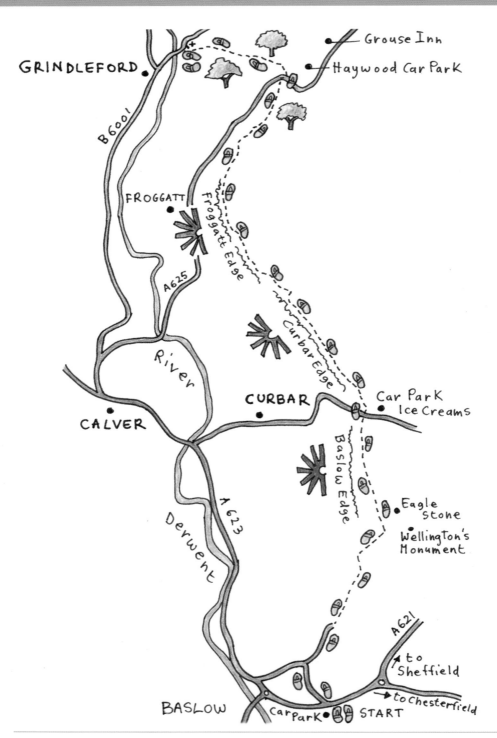

GRINDLEFORD

B6001

FROGGATT

A625

River

CALVER

Derwent

A623

Grouse Inn

Haywood Car Park

Froggatt Edge

Curbar Edge

CURBAR

Car Park
Ice Creams

Baslow Edge

Eagle
Stone

Wellington's
Monument

A621

to
Sheffield

to Chesterfield

BASLOW

Car Park   START

Grindleford
Froggatt
Calver
Baslow
The Edges
Grindleford

Distance: 10.1 miles

Starting Point: Grindleford Church

Follow route directions for:

Grindleford	Page 88
Froggatt	Page 92
Calver	Page 96

... until you reach the car park/village hall in Baslow village. **The return route is shown below.**

Standing outside the village hall, turn left and then cross over the main road using the pedestrian crossing.

Take the road up the side of the restaurant, Eaton Hill.

At the top, turn right and walk up Bar Road. This climbs high up and turns into a track.

Ignore any paths left or right and when you reach the top you see the Wellington Monument ahead to the right.

(At this point take the chance to visit the monument or to simply glance around at the magnificent views behind you.)

At the junction of paths take the main path bearing left.

Continue on this wide track along Baslow Edge.

Just before you reach the gate you will notice a gravel path to the left which leads to a fantastic viewpoint well worth a detour.

Back on track – go through the gate, cross over the road and go on the opposite path up to Curbar Edge.

(Note – if you turn right at the road to the car park, there is usually an ice cream van parked here.)

Go through the gate and take the main gravel path straight ahead along Curbar Edge.

You may wish to take advantage of diverting to the edge to see the most incredible views but take great care.

Curbar Edge path naturally runs into Froggatt Edge path and you just enjoy this simple path along the edges until you meet the road.

Go through the gate and walk up the road a few yards then cross over with great care (fast road!!) and go through the stile on the opposite side.

Follow the obvious path that leads to Haywood car park.

On the lower side of the car park, follow the footpath sign and head down hill to Nether Padley.

Go through the gate and head downhill through the wood.

Ignore any paths to the right and keep downhill eventually meeting a stone wall. Continue downhill with the wall on your right.

The path then veers to the right and the lane then leads down to Grindleford church.

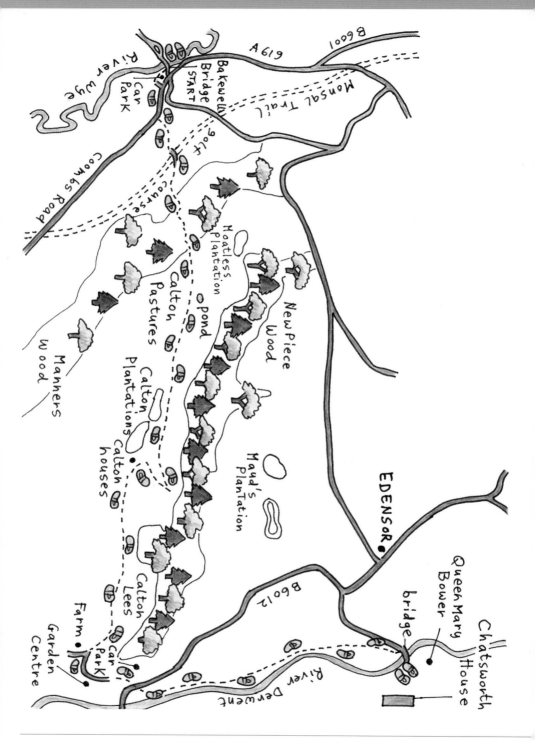

Chatsworth
Edensor
Bakewell
Calton Lees
Chatsworth

Distance: 8.35 miles

Starting Point: Chatsworth Bridge, below the House.

Follow route directions for:

... until you reach the bridge in Bakewell. **The return route is shown below.**

Standing on the bridge in Bakewell, you need to take the riverside footpath downstream with the river on your right and the car park on your left.

When you meet the road, turn left and after a few yards at the junction, turn right on to Coombs Road.

Walk along the pavement and when the houses end on the right hand side, cross over and take the public footpath sign on the opposite side, through the large gate and up to a long drive.

At the top, go through the gate and continue upwards.

As the drive curves to the left follow the thin gravel path off to the right that follows the wall up to the top corner.

Go over the bridge which looks down on the Monsal trail, and continue straight ahead towards the golf course (ignore 2 gates on the left).

Walk across the golf course without delay and then enter the woods.

Climb the obvious path up through the woods.

The path appears to split but keep left upwards, taking the rocky path climbing with care.

At the junction of the paths take the path opposite and continue to the top of the woods.

Go through the gate in the stone wall and enter the field bearing right uphill. Walk to the right side of the trees and head for the small gate straight ahead. Go through the gate with the pond on your left.

Bear left to another small gate signposted Chatsworth and go through to the field with a pond.

Head down the hill on the obvious path.

(Note this section now retraces your steps for a while but the views are glorious!)

Head for the gate at the bottom of the field and climb the stile into the next field.

Continue forwards until you reach a junction of paths (with the black and white Russian House ahead). Take the right path and head downhill with the wall on your left.

Go through the gate in the wall and follow the well defined path past Calton Lees Cottages. Keep on this track as it drops down the valley.

Continue forwards, eventually passing the Chatsworth Garden Centre on your right and the car park to your left.

Continue along the road until you meet the main road that runs through the Chatsworth Estate.

At the cattle grid, cross over with care and take the path that drops down to the river. Turn left and follow the riverside path all the way back to the bridge and continue on to Chatsworth House.

Chatsworth Photo: Graham Dunn

If you want a book printed

You need only phone, or email:

emma@northend.co.uk
copied to
ks@northend.co.uk

to receive helpful and friendly information

NORTHEND
CREATIVE PRINT SOLUTIONS

Printers of Fine Books since 1889 and winners of numerous awards

Clyde Road Sheffield S8 0TZ Tel: 0114 250 0331 Fax: 0114 250 0676 www.northend.co.uk

With Give as you Live™ you can turn every pound you spend online into funds for Tourism for All UK. Just visit http://www.tourismforall.org.uk/giveasyoulive.html to learn how you can raise an extra £75 this year, at no cost to you.

Tourism for All UK is the UK's central source of information and advice to the public when they are seeking accessible facilities and services. Tourism for All Services provides help and support to the tourism industry when businesses are trying to become more accessible. 100% of all profits generated from these activities help to support our information services to disabled and older people.

Tourism for All UK (TfA) provides information to disabled or older people on accessible accommodation and other tourism services in the UK and at selected overseas destinations. Every year they respond to thousands of people who may need help and support to enable them to take a break they may not have previously believed possible. Additionally, over 300,000 people have visited their website in the past 12 months.

TfA is a national registered charity, and its information service is backed by a website, www.tourismforall.org.uk, and supported by a helpline, 0845 124 9971. The aim is to provide lively, inspirational and comprehensive information that encourages people to try new things, see new places, and live life to the full!

As well as accommodation, travel, and attractions, TfA provides information about activity holidays for disabled people; equipment hire; places where care is available; escorts & carer services; and sources of finance towards the cost of a holiday for people on low income.

'OPENBRITAIN' is a recently introduced high quality guide published by Tourism for All UK with the support of the national tourist agencies VisitEngland, VisitScotland and VisitWales, and disability charity RADAR. It is also backed by AA, the British Hospitality Association, Disabled Go, and a host of other organisations. OpenBritain is packed with information about accessible tourism drawn from all these sources, and is the key resource for any disabled visitor. The guide costs £9.99, is available from bookshops from December, or can be purchased direct from Tourism for All. There is also a companion website: www.openbritain.net, where information about accessible accommodation can also be tracked down.

Brian Seaman

Having two disabled sons and having been a District Nursing Sister for 13 years in Derbyshire, I am acutely aware that accessibility is such an important issue.

With 32.7 million day visitors per year to Derbyshire, 10 million disabled in Britain and 87 million in Europe – the market is huge! Individuals with disabilities need to be catered for as a normal part of customer service.

Derbyshire is such a special place and has so many great days out for EVERYONE to enjoy.

Hire adapted bikes and cycle on the numerous trails, take to the waters with Sailability at Carsington Water, try abseiling at Millers Dale, enjoy swimming in Bakewell or strolling around the many beautiful villages.

A picnic at the viewpoint on Curbar/ Baslow Edge or a day spent at the fully accessible Chatsworth House gives memories to treasure forever. With new accessible trails being created go to www.visitpeakdistrict.com for details or view the 'You're Welcome' booklet from the Tourist Information Centre.

With the Olympics and Paralympics in 2012 Britain made a pledge to make venues throughout the country as accessible as possible. Derbyshire has been selected as a 'DESTINATION OF DISTINCTION', 91 minutes by train from London.

The following properties, although not all necessarily on the "Golden Miles Route", or in the National Accessibility Scheme may be suitable if you have a disability and wish to visit Derbyshire.

PLEASE, PLEASE check with the owners for details of their accessibility statements prior to booking...

Only those in the Scheme guarantee the provision of nationally agreed standards but suitable properties may be available that provide level access, downstairs bedrooms, bathrooms or wetrooms.

Disability varies so much but one of the main things to consider if you have a property accessible to the public is to make sure that everyone can get in, move around, be able to wash and go to the toilet!

Gillian Scotford

*Clark&Partners*Ltd

Mobility & Agecare Centres

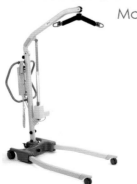

We are able to hire moving and handling equipment along with manual wheelchairs throughout the Yorkshire and Derbyshire region to enable access.

Clark & Partners Ltd

1 Orgreave Way, Sheffield, S13 9LS

Tel: 0114 229 3388

Web: www.clarkandpartners.co.uk

Useful Information

Holiday accommodation within Derbyshire with level access, downstairs bedroom and bathroom (some wet rooms) that may be suitable if you have a disability.

Great Longstone	Thornbridge Manor	www.thornbridgemanor.co.uk
Cressbrook	Cressbrook Hall	www.cressbrookhall.co.uk
Froggatt	Jemima Lodge	www.letsstay.co.uk
Chatsworth	Chatsworth Caravan Club	www.caravanclub.co.uk
Brassington	Hoe Grange Holidays**	www.hoegrangeholidays.co.uk
Wirksworth	Pott's cottage	www.chatsworth.org
Rowsley	East Lodge Hotel**	www.eastlodge.com
Ilam	Cottage by the pond	www.beechenhill.co.uk
Matlock	Pear Tree Farm Guest House	www.derbyshirearts.co.uk
Ashbourne	Sandybrook Park	www.pinelodgeholidays.co.uk
Darley Dale	Darwin Forest	www.pinelodgeholidays.co.uk
Monyash	Rowson House	www.rowsonhousefarm.com
Near Buxton	Sheldon Cottage	www.wheeldontreesfarm.co.uk
Newhaven	The Piggery	www.oldhousefarm.com
Near Ashbourne	Peak District Spa	www.peakdistrictspa.co.uk
Near Ashbourne	Rivendale Caravan Park	www.rivendalecaravanpark.co.uk
Hartington	Whitehouse Farm Barn	www.whitehousefarmbarn.co.uk
Ashover	Holestone Moor Barns	www.hmbarns.co.uk
Near Buxton	The Seven Room	www.stoopfarm.co.uk
Near Hope	Farfield Farm	www.farfieldfarmcottages.co.uk
Hartington	Ashtree Cottage	www.netttorfarm.co.uk
Brushfield	Middle Farm Holiday Cotts	www.middlefarmholidaycottages.co.uk
Near Chesterfield	Red Lion	www.redlionandbistro.com
Holmesfield	Gooseberry Barn	www.gooseberryfarmcottages.co.uk
Haddon	Haddon Grove	www.haddongrovefarmcottages.co.uk
Near Castleton	Rushop Hall	www.rushophall.com
Ashbourne	Ashbourne Hall	www.ashbourneselfcatering.com
Wormhill*	Hargate Hall	www.hargate-hall.co.uk
Hope	Gypsy's Barn	www.peakdistrictholidaycottages.com

The following holidays are suitable for people with learning disabilities:

Foolow	Mountain House	www.mountain-house.co.uk
Near Matlock	Lea Green Activity Centre	www.derbyshire.gov.uk

* Check star rating
** Award Winning
Highlighted text businesses are on "The Golden Miles" Route.